OUTBOUND TELEPHONE SELLING

Outbound Telephone Selling

A management manual

Pat Cochrane

Gower

Published by
Gower Publishing Limited
Gower House
Croft Road
Aldershot
Hampshire GU11 3HR
England

Gower
Old Post Road
Brookfield
Vermont 05036
USA

Pat Cochrane has asserted her right under the Copyright, Designs and Patents Act 1988 to be identified as the author of this work.

British Library Cataloguing in Publication Data
Cochrane, Pat
    Outbound telephone selling : a management manual
    1. Telephone selling   2. Telemarketing
    I. Title
    658.8'4

    ISBN 0 566 08089 3

Library of Congress Cataloging-in-Publication Data
Cochrane, Patricia M., 1949—
    Outbound telephone selling : a management manual / Patricia M. Cochrane
        p.   cm.
    ISBN 0-566-08089-3 (hardcover)
    1. Telephone selling.   I. Title.
HF5438.3.C625   1999   99-24996
658.8'4—dc21   CIP

Typeset in 10 point Palatino by IML Typographers, Chester and printed in Great Britain at the University Press, Cambridge.

Contents

Preface

Since the early 1960s newspapers in the UK have been happily engaged in the profitable and cost-effective exercise of outbound telephone selling. They have long recognized that customers are willing to buy from salespeople provided the approach is professional and targeted appropriately. Face-to-face contact proved to be unnecessary to achieve substantial sales revenue. However, so unrecognized was this form of sales and marketing activity, that as a telephone sales manager at the *Guardian* in the early 1980s, the usual response from people outside the publishing world to my explanation of what I did was: 'So what kind of telephones do you sell, then?'

Traditionally companies have relied on field sales teams to maintain adequate sales contact with customers. This is an expensive way to do business especially as customers today are comfortable doing business via the telephone. Think about the last time that you wrote a letter and the last time that you made a telephone call to communicate your personal and business needs. Shocking, isn't it, how much we rely on the telephone to hurry things along. Sustaining large teams of administrators to handle written enquiries from customers is time-consuming and unsatisfactory for customers. Customer service teams who handle such queries via the telephone are well established and successful. They speed up and improve the business process because problems can be solved much more quickly. Complex orders, queries and negotiations can be handled in a telephone conversation as effectively as in a face-to-face meeting. Therefore it is a logical next step for any company to expand the use of the telephone as a means of achieving sales.

I have been prompted to write this book because in the last 10 years I have seen a significant change in attitude towards telephone selling from 'we don't do that' to 'how do we do that' when the subject of proactive telephone contact with customers is raised. This change of attitude has been influenced by the need to cut sales costs and the introduction of technology that supports the sales function and makes it easier for customers to do business via the telephone. We live in a telephone-friendly culture which has seen the use of the telephone emerge as a significant tool of communication between companies and their customers.

The growth of telephone selling has also been driven by the desire to improve the quality of service offered to customers. New telephone technology, which allows companies to integrate telephone activity with computerized customer records, has forced the pace and stimulated companies into re-assessing how they sell to existing and prospective customers. Customers are more willing than ever to buy goods and services via the telephone. This is indicated by the phenomenal growth in the use of 0800 and other freephone or premium numbers. Paradoxically, whilst companies have embraced the use of inbound lines to establish contact with their customers, there is still a reluctance to make outbound calls. This has primarily been because telephone selling has suffered from an image problem created by the unscrupulous sales tactics of companies who have gone for the quick kill. One director of a high street bank was reluctant to engage in proactive outbound telephone activity because he was anxious to avoid upsetting the bank's customers. His reluctance was founded on his own experience of receiving unsolicited calls from double-glazing salespeople and his reaction to their unprofessional tactics. The same director was amazed to discover that when the bank tentatively embarked on an outbound telephone initiative to inform customers of the full range of services on offer, customers who had used the bank for 20 years, were unaware that it offered mortgages! Expensive campaigns in the press, personal advisors in the bank, mailshot campaigns and numerous other promotion activities could not achieve what a conversation on the telephone did in a few minutes. The bank now has a structured telephone programme that starts with a welcome call to every new customer.

This story also underlines, as does the case study of BT's outbound call initiative in Chapter 3, that telephone selling to consumers in their own home can be very successful when there is already a relationship between the company and the customer. Customers are receptive to receiving calls from companies that they already do business with because it underlines the commitment of the company to the customer. People like to do business with people who like to do business with them. Direct mail programmes are enhanced when the mailing is followed up with a telephone call and an increase in business from customers is guaranteed. A follow-up call can do something that no mailing no matter how carefully it is thought out can achieve – it allows the customer to interact with a company; it allows the customer to ask questions. Passively waiting for customers to contact a company will not maximize the sales opportunities that a mailing programme will stimulate. Whilst customers are encouraged to contact telephone helplines and order departments via the telephone, in some companies the focus remains firmly on reactive rather than proactive calls. Five years ago virtually the only advertiser on television to use a freephone telephone number to attract response from viewers was a national charity. Today every kind of company is represented from financial services to soft drinks. This demonstrates a lack of telephone phobia on the part of customers but it is not reflected in a similar growth in outbound telephone selling. However, where such activity is engaged in it invariably exceeds all expectations.

This book will answer the questions that are most frequently asked by companies and individuals whether they are about to introduce outbound calls into the sales mix or want to develop their current telephone activities:

- What are the benefits of using the telephone to achieve a sale?
- What sort of people should I recruit?
- Will my existing team successfully make the transition from inbound to outbound calls?
- How can I assist the process?
- What sort of calls should we be making?
- How can we improve our present performance?
- Will our customers buy without seeing someone face-to-face?
- How do you sell on the telephone?

As well as answers to these questions you will also be supplied with training material and ideas that can be easily adapted to your individual and company needs. Transcripts and detailed analysis of the structure of an outbound telephone call will provide a firm foundation for the practice of professional telephone selling. Chapter 6 will focus on helping you to develop advanced skills that will be required by those who engage in complex negotiations with customers as well as offering some new ideas for handling frequently voiced concerns from customers.

The techniques demonstrated in the book will enable new and experienced sales professionals to approach the task of telephone selling with confidence. It also includes case studies from companies who have already taken this step and you can learn from their experience. Whether you are a practitioner, a manager or thinking of stretching your company's telephone expertise to make the most of every business opportunity that can be generated via the telephone, this book will help you to achieve your goals.

Acknowledgements

I would like to thank all the telephone salespeople and managers who made time in their busy schedules to contribute information about their experience. Their help in highlighting the merit of a structured, professional approach to outbound telephone selling was invaluable. In particular, I reserve a special mention for Moria Rule, Catherine Hacker, Therese Eltringham and Ann Ainslie.

Introduction: the business benefits of outbound telephone sales

Finding, gaining and keeping customers

Unless a company is constantly looking for new customers either to replace the ones who have chosen a new supplier or to expand its customer base it will become stagnant. Customers' businesses are dynamic and change is occurring all the time. It is risky to adopt a reactive stance to customer needs. Customers vote with their feet if their needs are not met and you may leave it too late to rectify a problem that has resulted in a disgruntled customer. It makes sense to identify and rectify problems before they become insurmountable. Relationships with customers must be proactive. If customers feel they are taken for granted they may go elsewhere, especially if you are in a very competitive market. Customers may choose another supplier for all sorts of reasons, some of which you may be able to correct through proactive contact. Among those reasons might be the following:

- Your competitors are offering better products or services than you can provide.
- Your competitors are pricing similar products and services for less than you sell them.
- Your sales contacts leave a company and a new broom sweeps in with its own preferred suppliers.
- Your customers' loyalty has been taken for granted.
- Changes in a customer's business has created needs of which you are unaware.

It does not necessarily mean that the company has failed if a customer goes elsewhere but it does mean that some sort of strategy to find new customers needs to be in place to counteract the loss of business. As well as identifying new business opportunities your strategy should also include consolidating your relationship with existing customers.

The proliferation of freephone numbers is an indication of the commitment of companies to provide an easy route for customers to gain access to information about products and services and to place orders quickly and easily. Companies know that if they make it easy for their customers to purchase it increases the likelihood of a sale. The telephone is the ideal medium to develop relationships with customers and address customer concerns before they become serious problems. The telephone allows companies to maintain regular contact with customers without the burden of funding expensive personal visits. It costs five times as much to find a new customer as it does to keep the ones that you already have. Therefore companies have embarked on expensive customer care programmes to ensure that their relationships with customers are nurtured. Customers are made to feel that their business is valued. Now it is time to go beyond customer service and actively look for ways to increase your sales to existing customers and search out new ones. It is a simple step to progress from reactive inbound response handling to proactive outbound calling to identify more sales opportunities. If customers do not call you to place an order it is not necessarily because they do not wish to purchase. They may mean to call but don't get around to it. Outbound calling closes this gap in the sales process. Think of all the times you have collected money-off coupons and stored them in a kitchen drawer. Yet despite the attractiveness of the offer and the money it will save, you never use them. Eventually, after they have clogged up the drawer for some time, are curly and yellow with age and beyond their redemption date, you throw them out. Such promotions rely on the inertia of customers to avoid full redemption which might render the offer too expensive for the company to fund. Similarly, mailings, brochures and other literature sent out to customers may stimulate interest. The material may even be neatly stored away 'on file' for future reference. Unfortunately the customer does not follow through with any action. It is this customer inertia that outbound calling seeks to overcome. If a call is made to the customer the interest that has been stimulated can be progressed to a successful sale by a telephone salesperson.

Customers often buy from companies whilst remaining unaware of the full range of products and services that a company can offer. Maximizing the opportunity to sell to customers is not the main focus of a customer service team and so sales opportunities may be lost. For example a customer may have a complaint resolved satisfactorily but the call ends without the employee seeking the customer's commitment to further purchases. If customers have experienced problems in the delivery or performance of goods or services it will help if you speak to them before they have to contact you to complain. This will give you the opportunity to solve the problem before it escalates into a crisis. Outbound 'customer service' calls should be sales-oriented so that as well as consolidating a relationship with your customers you also make the most of the sales opportunity.

Companies are now reassessing the role of field selling in their marketing plans. The cost of maintaining a face-to-face contact with customers is expensive with no guarantee of a return on your investment. Therefore it makes sense to focus the effort of the field sales team where it is likely to yield the most profitable results. This usually means concentrating on gaining new customers (via qualified appointments, not cold-calling) or managing the accounts of key customers. Whilst developing close relationships with key customers is essential, sometimes accounts are serviced by field salespeople when they could be equally managed by telephone. Alternatively, if a field salesperson is primarily rewarded for the acquisition of new business rather than customer retention, the needs of existing customers may be sacrificed to the prospecting activities of the salesperson. Difficulties also occur when a customer requests a visit from a salesperson who will not be in the customer's area for several weeks. Often this need for a visit can be handled by telephone and indeed this may be the way the field salesperson actually deals with the customer's query. Telephone account management allows field salespeople to concentrate on those customers whose queries need their physical presence either for demonstration or for technical reasons.

When deciding what customer accounts should be managed by the internal sales team customers should be allocated for sound well-researched reasons and not arbitrary instinctive impulses. It does not necessarily follow that customers who spend more with a company are the ones that require face-to-face contact or whose relationship with the company would be jeopardized if someone else managed the account. Often senior managers and 'decision-makers' in an organization are too busy to see a company representative unless there is a specific reason to do so and they may appreciate the convenience of having routine contact with a company by telephone rather than via expensive, time-consuming meetings.

Cutting the cost of a sale

Using the telephone to qualify appointments for field salespeople will ensure that their time is spent productively and will increase the number of sales that are closed. The cost of a visit can run into hundreds of pounds and unproductive calls waste the time of the customer and the salesperson. Prospecting for new business is essential, it is also the most expensive part of the sales process because it is unlikely that the first contact will produce a sale. It would be nice if every contact with a customer resulted in more business for the company but this does not happen, even on the telephone!

To maximize the results from a sales visit you can qualify appointments for the fields sales force by making outbound telephone calls to:

- Research how the buying process works in the customer's organization and identify who the salesperson should see;
- establish what potential there is to do business – is there a need?
- identify the competition;
- find out when the customer is likely to purchase;
- establish what the customer thinks of your company's product or service;
- ask how much the customer is buying. A visit for one item will be less profitable than a visit to a company which purchases a high volume;
- discover the anticipated budget available. If the customer's funds are limited a visit may not be appropriate.

All of the above information can be gained from a telephone conversation and will allow the external sales force to prioritize its activities and plan its sales diary much more efficiently. It will also facilitate good relationships between the external and internal teams if there is a clear understanding of what the field sales team expects or wants from an appointment. A 'contract' between the two teams will avoid conflict. For example some sales directors will feel that the opportunity to meet key decision-makers in an organization is reason enough. Their sales force will then utilize its sales skills to identify needs once it is face-to-face with customers. Others will feel that unless a need has already been identified the call is a waste of time. There are arguments in favour of both approaches, but the important point is to reach agreement before the call activity begins so that both teams understand their call objectives.

Of course, the sale can be closed over the telephone without any external visits. Even where the product or service is complex, if the telephone salesperson is knowledgeable customers will buy from someone they haven't actually met. Outbound selling has proved effective in a diverse range of businesses some of which are listed below.

Distribution services	Travel
Computers and computer consumables	Building supplies
Financial services	Electronic components
Advertising	Printing
Paper and flour mills	Consumer goods
Publishing	Flowers
Architectural supplies	Cable television

This small list gives a flavour of the diversity of companies who are using the telephone proactively to sell. Really there is no limit to the type of organization that will benefit from outbound telephone sales activity. Outbound sales calls will enable you to maximize the return on your marketing, advertising and promotional campaigns. Be proactive not reactive.

This book is designed to help companies and those engaged in outbound sales activities to overcome their inhibitions and develop the skills necessary to achieve success. To avoid mistakes it is useful to identify what it is about telephone selling that customers don't like. If you know the pitfalls you can avoid them!

Common negative misconceptions of telephone selling:

- It is intrusive. There is an assumption that customers will feel unhappy about being contacted.
- Telephone salespeople do not listen. Customers do not want to be harangued by over-zealous salespeople. One-sided conversations are very boring for the person who is not doing the talking.
- Selling is manipulative, salespeople use questionable sales techniques to extract a 'yes' from the customer. It is impossible to be ethical and sell.
- Salespeople persist beyond a point that is acceptable to customers. Sometimes the art of selling is knowing when no means no. Pursuing the unpursuable is unrewarding and wastes everyone's time.
- Salespeople are poorly trained. Companies can underestimate the training that is required to conduct telephone sales professionally. This applies to sales training and to product training. There is a misconception that telephone salespeople do not need as much training as field salespeople.
- Salespeople use dubious tactics to get through to the customers they wish to speak to. No one is impressed by the 'personal call' or the claiming of non-existent relationships with the prospect or customer.

However, these negative aspects can be eliminated by investing time and resources to ensure that your sales team is properly trained. The advantages of telephone selling outweigh the disadvantages. Aim for the 'can do' (or even 'must do') strategy rather than finding reasons, often spurious, not to sell via the telephone.

Advantages of selling via the telephone:

- It speeds up the buying process, thus creating more turnover. If you make it hard for your customers to buy you will lose business to your competitors who make it easy. Fewer sales opportunities will be missed when you increase the level and frequency of contact with your customers. Questions from the customer can be answered immediately without waiting for the next time that a salesperson is 'in the area'.

- It does not have geographical barriers. Your sales team can be in Scotland one minute and Europe the next. Sales time is maximized because no time is wasted travelling from one destination to the next. Location of the team does not have to be fragmented. You can set up a team wherever the location is most convenient for you.
- It helps to create stable and profitable relationships with customers. The more frequent the contact that you have with your customers the more opportunity you will have to explore the sales possibilities that exist for your company. You can establish relationships at all levels in the company from end-users of your product or service to senior decision-makers in the organization.
- It develops expertise. Talking to many customers accelerates the learning and understanding of your salespeople, thus making them more effective in their role. Telephone salespeople will engage in more sales calls per day than most field salespeople will do in a month.
- It is more cost-effective than face-to-face contact with customers. A telephone sales call will identify those customers who have a need for your product or service far more efficiently than cold-calling whilst out on field sales visits. Cost per field visit can be up to a hundred times as high as the equivalent telephone sales call. Telephone marketing will qualify calls for field salespeople which will ensure that more of their calls are effective, that is they call at the right time, they see the right person, they have the right product or service to offer. In addition, any sales that can be closed via the telephone without a visit from a salesperson will ensure that costs per sale are kept low.
- If you have an extensive customer base or a large target market that cannot be adequately covered by a field sales force, telephone selling will help you to fill the gap. Too long a time lapse between visits can erode a customer's loyalty and leave them open to the charms of your competitors. Cement relationships with your customers by ensuring that they have frequent and timely telephone contact from you.

1 The management and organization of telephone selling

How to recruit the right people or re-focus existing employees

Can anyone sell on the telephone? Yes, they can! In this chapter I hope to dispel a few myths about selling on the telephone. First of all, selling is a skill not an innate gift. It can be learned. As in any other business activity competence comes with practice and knowledge. The degree of professionalism that is required is just as great for selling as for any other business or professional activity. Whilst selling is a generic skill (its principles and practice can be applied to any business) a knowledge and understanding of a company's products, service, market and customers will be necessary to convince customers that your salespeople speak with authority and creditability. If your market is high-tech or specialized then your telephone salespeople will need to understand what the company's products or services can do before they can sell them successfully.

Case history

A national company that had highly qualified and experienced national account managers to service its top customers decided to supplement its account managers' sales efforts with telephone account management. The team's role was to 'sell in' products and services that had been sold at national level in their customers' companies. The team was set up quickly and it was felt that to ensure maximum success at the earliest opportunity only those who had previous telephone sales experience would be recruited. The resulting team presented a diverse mix of talent and ability. The team was to sell to information technology managers operating at a senior level in their companies. To maintain credibility with customers national account managers invariably had gained degrees in related subjects. The idea of an account manager, approaching customers without any idea of what the products did was unthinkable, yet because telephone contact was deemed as a lesser activity the same caution did not apply. The sales experience of the new telephone sales team included selling timeshare properties, double-glazing, recruitment advertising and employment agency services. None had received formal sales training. The company allowed telephone contact with its most important customers to be conducted by people who had no experience of its products, market or the needs of its customers, coupled with sales techniques gained in areas that did not develop long-term relationships with customers.

Turnover in the company proved high because the people the company recruited did not have the knowledge and skills to ensure their success. Targets were not met and the team became demoralized. Team members felt that their managers' expectations were unrealistic. The management team was disappointed because it felt that the new recruits had oversold their capacity to deliver a target-hitting performance.

What they did

The company took the following remedial steps:

- It redefined the job description so that the emphasis was now on knowledge and experience of the company's products and services.
- It focused on recruiting people who had a positive 'can do' attitude.
- It included enhanced product knowledge training in its induction programme so that the team fully understood the specific features and benefits the company had to offer to the customer.
- It developed a sales skills programme that introduced the team to the concept of a 'structured sale'.
- Initial induction training was followed up by the team leaders who were responsible for providing on-the-job coaching. This ensured that the team's sales skills were constantly reinforced by action planning which was designed to enhance the performance of all members of the team.

Learning points

Recruit people who have knowledge and experience of your products, services and market. Then develop their sales skills so that they communicate effectively with your customers. If you recruit employees who do not have the knowledge that you require then you must make room in your induction process for appropriate training to be given. This is only possible when the level of knowledge that is required is easily transferable.

Recruiting the right people

Are salespeople born or made? Any parent knows how persuasive children can be when they really want something. Selling, that is the ability to identify needs or wants and to persuade others that a product or service will match those needs and wants, is a skill that we utilize when we seek to influence others. We could be being interviewed, suggesting a night out to a friend or proposing a new way to carry out a business process. Attitude affects the ability to sell, so that if a proposition is made in a positive manner, people, that is customers, are more inclined to accept it. Our attitude is formed by the culmination of life experiences, culture and education. It is not easy to change people's attitude through training alone unless you have almost unlimited time to affect the change, something that is unlikely in today's business environment. If individuals have a positive attitude they are more likely to succeed at selling. Therefore it follows that the key to recruiting the right people is to look for those individuals who have a positive attitude. Sales skills can be transferred to those who have never sold providing they are willing to change their *behaviour* and practise the required skills to increase their expertise.

Appropriate training can be given to help new recruits to sell and communicate with their customers in a way that is persuasive and compelling. Most inexperienced salespeople or new recruits suffer from lack of confidence (increased when they are also new to the product or service that you want them to sell) and it is this, rather than a lack of ability, that prevents them from succeeding. Confidence can be gained through practice, experience on the job and the realization that 'selling' is an intrinsic part of how ideas and needs are communicated, and not exclusive to it. The ability to 'sell' is a life skill as well as a professional skill. When candidates are interviewed for a job they instinctively 'sell' their ability; they focus on what they do well, not their weaknesses. Experienced salespeople are not necessarily your best option. You will need to investigate what kind of sales training candidates have had and whether their approach to selling is compatible with your own. There is a risk that without proper exploration of their experience you might find that the sales tactics used by your new recruits are dubious and unprofessional. This could create a serious problem if a salesperson's attitude towards your customers is not what is desired. Customers may be appalled by the tactics of such recruits and this can threaten to destroy a company's credibility with highly valued customers. You could experience all of the following because of a poor attitude to customers:

- Promises are made to customers that cannot be fulfilled, for example delivery times.
- Unrealistic expectations are raised with regard to the level of service a

customer can expect, for example immediate call out when the reality is five working days.

- Disregard is shown for the terms and conditions of a contract, for example early termination clauses and how they affect the customer.
- Orders are progressed on unreliable information from the salesperson, for example the sale is not confirmed by the customer or the wrong products and services are ordered.
- There is a lack of adequate follow-up from the salesperson to ensure that customers are satisfied with the product or service they have bought.
- Inadequate attention is given to matching customers' needs, for example customers buy something that they cannot afford or that is incompatible with what they already have.

It is more appropriate to recruit people with the right attitude and who possess a knowledge of your market sector and then train them in sales skills. People who possess 'the right attitude' are those who display the following attributes:

1   A positive outlook.
2   Good interpersonal skills.
3   A desire to meet the needs of customers.

The process of recruitment

You may wish to recruit one new member of staff or several hundred. Almost certainly you will wish to spend your limited time wisely. Conducting interviews is time-consuming. You can maximize the value of the interview and increase your chances of successfully appointing if you pre-screen via a telephone interview. No matter how well presented, a c.v. will not give an indication of how effective an individual is on the telephone. Use the telephone to screen individuals before making a commitment to interview them in person. Do not conduct a formal interview on the telephone, rather frame your questions to gain a feel for the person at the other end of the telephone. At this stage what you are looking to establish is the following:

- Do they project confidence?
- Can they be clearly understood?
- Are they good listeners?
- Why are they interested in your job?
- Can they engage in conversation and make meaningful contributions to it?

Keep your questions open to encourage the free flow of information and make notes of the candidate's answers. The following examples are useful:

- What attracted you to this post?
- What is your current position?
- Tell me what you enjoy most about your current role.
- Describe your biggest success.
- What characteristics do you think you must possess to succeed at selling?

Keep the telephone interview brief. It is not intended to replace the personal interview. Ten minutes is plenty of time to get a good idea of the suitability of the candidate and enable you to make a decision on whether to interview him or her. Don't feel pressurized into making an instant decision, review your notes when all the calls have been completed and make your selection from them. You can advise candidates that if they have been successful they will hear from you in 24 hours. This will avoid the necessity to inform unsuccessful candidates in writing and thus save you even more time, and applicants will know whether they have been successful without having to wait for a formal reply from you.

Re-focusing existing staff

I handle incoming calls for the company I work for. I have been asked if I would consider doing outbound calls. This fills me with a little bit of apprehension. I am considering it but I really don't think it's going to happen. The problem is basically how I feel about doing this. It makes me feel very uncomfortable, approaching people as opposed to their approaching me. I'm ready to give information I have from questions that are asked of me but I really don't like the boot being on the other foot, me having to ask the questions and collate information to make a sale. I'd rather customers came to me. I feel at a disadvantage when I ring them because I've got to ask them for something. I quite enjoy the job I'm doing now because they're asking me and so I'm in control from that point of view. I can say yes or no and answer the questions using all my information. I don't have to go probing, which I think will make me feel uncomfortable.

This quote is from a company employee who takes incoming enquiries from prospective and existing customers which could lead to bookings for in-house and external training courses on computer software and hardware. The feelings expressed are typical of the trepidation experienced by individuals who are about to engage in proactive telephone activity. It could be argued that selling, whether face-to-face or on the telephone, has long been underrated as a business activity. Myths of spoilt salespeople only interested in their company car and commission have fuelled negative perceptions. This is exacerbated by the unscrupulous sales tactics adopted by some direct salespeople. Yet its most vociferous critics probably buy happily via the telephone unaware that they are engaged in a sales process as, for example, when they purchase holidays, book theatre tickets and contact company telemarketing and helplines. This negative view of selling is also held by individuals who are perfectly happy to communicate with customers when they are responding to incoming enquiries but are deeply fearful of instigating contact with customers. They are confident and competent and use sales skills to convert enquiries into sales or resolve customers' problems but feel that to initiate this process is somehow wrong. When companies introduce outbound telephone contact they can find that their employees are resistant to such initiatives.

It is important to reassure employees that it is perfectly possible to sell and be ethical at the same time. Professional salespeople look to establish long-term relationships with their customers. Recruiting salespeople who are one hit wonders is not the recipe for the continuing success of a company and companies readily acknowledge this. When customers buy they want reassurance that they are making the right decision for themselves or for their company. The source of the reassurance, that is the salesperson, will influence their decision. Most people feel confident that they can spot insincerity and if salespeople indulge in questionable tactics or manipulative techniques they will quickly be rejected by customers. If employees have reservations about engaging in proactive selling they are not likely to be successful until their own fears have been alleviated.

It is possible to help existing staff who are service rather than sales-oriented to sell successfully. If they are experiencing problems it is likely these stem from a negative attitude towards selling created by its reputation of being something that is manipulative. Often employees feel that selling is somehow morally reprehensible, typified by the following comment from a customer service helpline advisor: 'I only want to do the best I can for customers', implying that selling would not allow him to do 'the best' for customers. There may also be a fear of rejection by customers, after all if customers call the company they have initiated the communication and are unlikely to refuse to speak to someone, which may happen if the employee initiates the contact. This negative attitude has not been helped by companies who have adopted a rigid approach to selling and insist that their employees adhere to scripts and a prescribed format. The essence of successful selling on the telephone is that individuals should feel comfortable with what they are saying. If a script is inhibiting, it is time to ditch it.

A company should invest in training employees who are willing to try selling. If the employee's attitude is right the rest will follow. Telephone selling can be best summed up as 'If you want to do it you can, if you don't want to do it you won't.' Employees who claim that they could never sell on the telephone simply have not practised enough. Skills can only be acquired if the desire to learn them is there. Skill levels will increase with hard work, experience and practice.

If you about to introduce proactive calls into the marketing mix do not underestimate the importance of allowing enough time and opportunities for discussing these issues with the team. This will also enable you to direct your training activities where they are most needed. To get the debate going ask questions like these:

- What is selling?
- What was the last big purchase that you made?
- What influenced your decision to buy?
- What did the salesperson do that impressed you?
- Of those companies or products that you rejected, what did the salesperson do to reinforce your decision not to buy?
- Was there anything that the salesperson didn't do that would have made a difference?
- How important is price?
- What is the difference between price and value?
- What is the worst thing that can happen when you telephone a customer?
- What do you fear most when you speak to customers?
- What can we do to help you feel more confident?

The debate should help you to draw out issues that the team feels strongly about and enable you to counteract the negative perceptions. In particular the discussion should provide a platform for you to:

- present the positive aspect of selling, that it is about finding the right solution for the customer;
- discover the strengths and weaknesses of the team;
- identify training needs;
- reassure team members that you will provide appropriate support for them in their new role.

Keep a record of the main points of the discussion and use this as a basis for your action plan. Communicate the plan to the team and allow team members to input their own ideas. Once the plan is written follow it through!

The sales skills of the team

Many sales opportunities are lost because sales teams forget to practise the basic principles of selling. It is not enough to know the theory, it has to be applied. A structured approach to training from the point of induction and beyond will ensure that skills are regularly reviewed and updated. Training is only effective if the learning is consistently reinforced, and this does not mean 'programming'. Telephone selling is more effective when salespeople's spontaneity and individuality is fostered and encouraged. However, even highly skilled communicators can 'forget' to ask for a sale! On-the-job coaching will highlight areas where the telephone salesperson can improve or develop existing sales skills.

Start with essentials and as your salespeople become more confident and knowledgeable about the company you can introduce more advanced techniques such as negotiating and handling objections. Sales skills incorporate not just the structure of a call but communication and interpersonal skills. In particular, telephone salespeople need to focus on the advantages of using the telephone to communicate to customers and learn how to use their voices to project confidence and authority.

Keep meticulous training records so that you and the trainee can map progress. They will also provide evidence of your commitment to improving the trainee's performance and help you to deliver programmes that match the needs of the team. Training is only motivational when it is relevant.

The team's knowledge and understanding of the business

To have credibility with customers, salespeople need a thorough grounding in the product or service that they are selling. This may sound obvious but while companies may give adequate training in sales skills, too often not enough time is invested in enhancing salespeople's knowledge of the market in which they operate. Further, it is common for salespeople to sell products to customers that they themselves have *never seen*. Sales opportunities will be missed if the salesperson cannot help customers to visualize the advantages and benefits of a product or service. Telephone sales teams may be situated on a site far from the manufacturing process or the point of delivery to customers. If it is not practical to send all the team on field visits then send someone who can communicate the experience to the rest of the team when back at home base. A simple solution is to video company sites; an amateur video is perfectly adequate.

Supplement this knowledge with visits to key customers so that salespeople can see the product or service being used in situ. This will also help them to gain insight into customers' motivation to purchase. One sales director argued that her company did not require its telephone salespeople to have too much knowledge as customer questions could be answered by field salespeople when they met the customers. However, customers are unlikely to agree to a meeting suggested by someone who doesn't know what they are talking about, and dealing appropriately with questions from customers is often the influencing factor in helping a customer to decide whether or not to agree to a meeting.

Although it is true to say that once the customer's interest has been aroused then it is time to suggest a meeting, it is also important to project the right image of your company. Telephone salespeople can talk to literally hundreds of customers each week so it makes sense to ensure that the impression that they convey is a professionally competent one. Inadequate responses to questions from customers diminishes the company in the eyes of the customer.

Technological and administrative support

The use of the telephone in the sales process has had one significant impact on business and that is the speed at which customers expect things to be done. When customers conclude a conversation and put the phone down, their expectation is that whatever has been agreed will be actioned immediately. They are not interested in the infrastructure of the company or whether the sales support department is overwhelmed with requests for quotes, information or other queries. If the support for the sales team is inadequate salespeople may communicate their dissatisfaction to customers: 'I'll **try** to get that in the post tonight if our post department will accept it, but they may not want to.'

To avoid conflict you must make opportunities for interested parties to communicate their priorities, difficulties and problems and allow for these to be resolved with goodwill from all parties. Sending out written quotations to all prospective and existing customers without any discrimination, that is to anybody that asks for one, will cause log jams and lead to work overload for administrative staff. Therefore priorities should be negotiated so that all parties understand the impact of their requests on others, and thus customers will not be kept waiting unnecessarily for information.

Technical requirements may take the form of adequate faxing and photo-copying resources or sophisticated computer systems. Your software can be off-the-shelf or customized. If you are thinking of buying software thought must be given to how accessible the screens are and the speed with which they can be called up. Information such as customer names and addresses can be assigned a mandatory input code but use these with care. Excessive mandatory inputs slow the sales process and salespeople saying 'I'm sorry I'm just waiting for the computer' to customers does not encourage free-flowing conversation. Beware of code fever – one company gave its team 600 separate codes for the inputting of information. Selecting the appropriate code during the call was not possible because there were so many choices. The team resolved this by taking handwritten notes during the call and inputting the codes when the call was finished. This had the effect of slowing down the process, not speeding it up as was originally intended – 600 codes cannot be memorized!

Your computer system may be inadequate and require upgrading to cope with the sales activity of the team. If you are in the process of upgrading ask the systems analysts to sit alongside the salespeople and observe at first hand what they are doing. If the analysts understand the sequence of the calls that the team is making then they will create screens that are in a systematic order and avoid salespeople having to jump from one screen to another. If the system is 'imposed' it will almost certainly not be user-friendly. A company that already had several computer systems decided to create a stand-alone computer system for its telephone sales team. The idea was to implement a system that was customized to the specific needs of the team so the IT department was asked to trawl the market to find a system that was the best match for the team's requirements. The IT department bought a system that was designed to support database management and brought in consultants to customize the system further to support the sales function. The system is slow (the server is too small to provide the speed the team needs to switch between screens) and there is no facility to access a 'snapshot' of the customer. No screen can provide basic information such as address, contacts, what the customer has now and a record of previous conversations in one easy to view format. The team has to access numerous menu bars and pop up screens to store and retrieve information, which is confusing and slow. The company asked the team to trial the new system *after* the purchasing decisions were made. Problems that have been identified by the team are now in the hands of the consultants who have said that they will not be able to resolve all of them. The team is not impressed.

Whilst a database management function is essential in any system (the team will gather information that can be used in marketing campaigns to stimulate the interest of customers), the point of contact between a salesperson and a customer, that is the telephone call, means that any system that you choose will have to be flexible, provide easy access to information and make inputting logical and sequential. Ask the team what it needs before you buy.

Integrate computer systems so that all relevant information is available to the team and install data management software.

When I was with my previous company we had to set up a pilot to specify what system we wanted. We started with a very simple database that you could quite easily do on any standard business database software. We ran with that for three months and during that time we identified what we actually needed. This allowed us to see whether we did need a fully blown telephone marketing system or whether we could take downloads from our existing customer database and use those. What we discovered was that while basic customer details on a database would be fine for some campaigns, we wanted to do a fully integrated marketing programme involving direct mail, response handling, different campaigns on different customer types and create different call lists. We wanted to take the customer all the way through from prospecting to converting them to being a customer to getting them over a certain spend level and then to maintaining that customer. So in order to do that you really did need a transactional database and a relationship database as well, so that's when we started looking at the different telephone marketing products on the market. We went all round Europe and the States and we finally settled on one from the States. We worked very closely with a consultant to get a bespoke package and we were lucky enough to be able to do what they called RAD, Rapid Application Design, and what that meant really was rather than having to write huge documents saying exactly what you needed the system to do in the nth degree, they would sit there and develop it with you, they would watch what you were doing and then they'd say this is what you need the system to do and they would develop the system alongside people who were doing the job. They sat amongst a telephone marketing team, watching what they were doing and they would make amendments to the system as they went along. The objectives of the call are, within the overall objective of customer loyalty, quite specific, they are to sell a certain number of products. The system identifies the person who phones the customer and what they have attempted to sell. There are codes on the first screen that say 'this is what you are going to speak to this customer about' and then as you just click through the system it will automatically bring up scripts for the products which you are selling.

Outbound telephone sales manager

One of the most frustrating experiences for a team is the lack of system support or the slowness of it. This is a technology problem which has no cheap answer. Upgrading and integrating technology is an expensive business and costly mistakes can be made. If it is not possible to provide total integration then it is important to consider what management and customer information the team will require access to and then to provide the means to access it even if initially this is a paper process. Records of contacts that the customer has had with the company that might be relevant to the content of the call, for example complaints, conversations with field salespeople, etc., should be available at the time of the call so that the salesperson is not at a disadvantage or unprepared for what the customer might say.

Before you purchase software, spend time with the team to identify what processes it is involved in, for example preparing quotations, maintaining diaries, etc., so that the specification is right. Involve salespeople in this process as the flow of a call can be ruined if a programmer has configured a system that does not reflect the structured approach to a call. This can lead to time-wasting conversations both for the team and the company's customers. A direct sales operation that provided home and motor insurance found that qualifying questions came at the end of its computerized script, leading to unproductive lengthy calls when it would have been better for both parties to discuss acceptability earlier in the call. Questions such as 'Have you been convicted of driving offences?' or 'Have you made a claim for household insurance in the last 12 months?' which were asked to establish whether a policy could be underwritten came at the end of a call. If it is true that refusal often offends it is certainly true that refusal is guaranteed to offend when a customer can reasonably reply 'Why didn't you ask me that earlier?'

Software that allows salespeople to generate their own diary call backs and correspondence does not have to be prohibitively expensive as one manager of a small team discovered:

> Our software is absolutely tremendous. As a system it does have its limitations, and given what I know now I would probably choose something a bit more sophisticated. We are ready to move on to the next step. But for the price (£200), for what it gives you, you can virtually eliminate paper from the process because every sales record is on it, it will give you your dialling lists, hot lists of people to call, it enables us to personalize standard letters and generate letters from it, it has just removed so much manual work.

Communication channels between all internal teams should be reviewed regularly so that any potential sources of irritation are dealt with quickly before they affect the customer. The telephone sales manager is pivotal, not peripheral, to rest of the organization and the management team. Telephone sales managers can become isolated and develop a defensive attitude if they perceive that their efforts and those of the team are undervalued.

A positive relationship between the internal sales team and the field sales force can be attained if proper consideration is given to the needs (sometimes conflicting) of both teams. Field sales teams may feel that their status is undermined by the introduction of telephone sales and fail to offer appropriate support and information. Telephone sales teams may imagine that the life of the external salesperson is one long round of socializing with customers. Failure to provide opportunities for feedback to each group will result in misunderstandings and internal wrangling which will be reflected in the perceptions and experiences of customers when they have contact with your organization.

The physical environment in which salespeople work

It is tempting to make do if space is at a premium, after all you only need a telephone, don't you? Unlike field salespeople who see different customers in different environments every day, telephone salespeople see the same four walls week in and week out and every effort should be made to make their surroundings stimulating and visually attractive. Walls provide a canvas for photographs, marketing information, sales graphs and performance records. If the walls look busy, the team looks busy. Consider practical issues such as the location of essential office equipment, for example fax machines. If other members of staff have to use them it will create opportunities for chatting which may disturb those on the telephone. Also, if telephone salespeople have to go to other locations or departments to use such equipment, it can be difficult to assess whether they are away from their desks for a good reason. Prolonged absences from a desk undermine efforts to maintain productivity and going to the post room provides a welcome excuse not to get on the telephone for those whose motivation is low.

Whether salespeople should sit facing each other, in groups or in isolation is another consideration. It is tempting to design office accommodation along utilitarian lines. Call centres, for example, which have to accommodate huge numbers of people are often arranged in formal and impersonal rows. However, it is difficult to generate team motivation and high office morale in these environments even when managers or team leaders constantly 'walk the floor'. You may wish to consider the impact on the motivation of the team before making any decisions. A favoured configuration is the 'star' shape where workstations are arranged so that a small group, usually eight people, is grouped around a central console facing inwards towards each other. This facilitates the need for human contact, other than that they get on the telephone, and team members can provide each other with mutual support.

How to organize your telephone selling for maximum efficiency

Create an efficient work environment

A salesperson was very upset when his sales director insisted that the salesperson cleaned out the company car while he watched to make sure that the salesperson did a thorough job. It used to be a widely held belief that field salespeople carried their customer records in the boot of their cars (or their heads) much to the consternation of internal sales support staff who were never quite sure what the customer had been promised when disagreements arose. Fortunately many of these problems have been eradicated with the introduction of lap top computers linked to the company's own computer to which all relevant parties have access. You may feel that the sales director was a little over the top. The salesperson certainly did. 'What's the problem?' he wailed. 'None of my customers see my car, what difference does it make?' Well, and this is the point, how organized and methodical an individual's and team's workspaces are is a reflection of their attitude to the job. It does not matter whether a customer can actually see them or not. Salespeople who work from home, for example, admit that if they are tempted to make calls wearing dressing gowns or sloppy casual wear it affects their confidence when talking to customers. To project competence and professionalism they have to feel right and that means they have to look right.

It is a myth that successful salespeople are not good administrators. They must be organized if they want to succeed at selling. Inefficiency and a disorganized approach to telephone selling will guarantee that they will miss sales opportunities.

Some companies have a more rigid approach to workspace than others. One company enforces a strict 'clean desk' policy where no personal possessions of any kind are allowed in the work area, even cold drinks are decanted into company paper cups decorated with the company's logo to maintain a consistency of image. No food is allowed at desks and a no paper policy is in force. Unfortunately one problem that the company does have is that its employees resist efforts to make them wear what the company deems to be appropriate business dress. People will find ways to assert their own ideas and personalities if they do not understand the rationale behind codes of dress and clean desk policies. Other companies have a much more relaxed view and express no objection to food being munched at desks, even when a member of the team may be called upon to speak to a customer whilst rapidly bolting down a lunchtime sandwich. A clean desk policy will enable the team to project a professional image to the rest of the company and customers who may visit the company from time to time. Facilities for tea and coffee should be out of sight and team members should be encouraged to eat away from their desks if this is possible. Nothing looks worse to visitors' eyes than the sight of lunch scattered over desks alongside packets of crisps, sweet wrappers and drinks. If you cannot provide separate dining facilities then limit the time food can be on desks. Aim for a compromise that encourages a relaxed, happy atmosphere and allows individuals to express themselves yet project a professional attitude.

Teams may be housed in a variety of office environments – old and modern. Some will be purpose-built such as BT's call centre, others will be sectioned off areas in departments that also conduct other business processes. Even where there may be budget constraints, here are a few practical ideas to improve surroundings:

1   Provide an adequate supply of drinks – telephone selling is thirsty work.
2   Organize sales support so that it comes to the team not the other way around.
3   Keep the office tidy and don't allow dumping from other departments, for example samples and brochures should not be stored under desks.
4   Allow personal touches but don't accept clutter.
5   Keep colours bright and try to create a light, airy atmosphere.
6   Put motivational material on the wall, for example photographs, leaderboards, press material, positive comments from customers.

7   Install the best telephone system that you can afford and provide head-
    sets.
8   Provide adequate storage space.

Take the long view – consolidate customer relationships

In a sales environment naturally the emphasis of all call activity is to maximize the number of sales that are possible. Stretching targets are set and the
performance of everyone in the department is measured by the achievement
of these targets. An over-reliance by salespeople on their regular customers
can mean that less 'important' customers, that is those that order less frequently, are neglected. Calls to customers that start with 'have you got
anything for me today' become the norm. Customers feel devalued and salespeople forget to sell them the benefits of the product or service. Eventually
this will lead to customers under-appreciating what your company can offer
and they will become susceptible to approaches from your competitors. It is
also possible to 'oversell' particularly if the pressure is on to hit targets, but
customers usually do not get bitten more than once. Short-term sales
strategies become firefighting strategies. Encourage your team to take the
long view and focus on consolidating relationships with customers that are
mutually trusting.

Give your team enough to do

The lack of available 'quality' leads is one of the most consistent gripes of
telephone sales teams. Of course, the definition of quality is subjective and
the gripes are not always justified. Call leads can range from grubby copies of
Yellow Pages to multi-million direct marketing campaigns to warm up existing and potential customers. Supplying good quality call material to the team
will increase the return that you get from its activity. Delegate the desk
research, for example cleaning the database, so that the team can focus on
selling, as this marketing manager would agree:

> Of course, one of the most important things is the quality of the leads that the tele-
> phone sales staff are following up. You have to think about how you are going to
> generate their activity. That's very important. Ask yourself how you keep them
> adequately and fruitfully employed with good quality leads, prospects or material.
> It has to be very good quality. Whether it's targeted mail campaigns or whether
> you 're cross-selling to existing customers, you need to make sure the profiling is
> done correctly so that they have the most chance of success.

Keep communication between interested groups open and accessible

Invite guests from other departments into your meetings with the sales team.

Provide a platform for contributions from the team and from others so that potentially controversial topics can be aired. For example a new process in the accounts department may have an adverse effect on customers which is then communicated to the sales team. If the team understands why the process has been changed the team will be more effective at handling enquiries from customers. Encourage feedback from the field sales force to the telephone sales team so that appointments that have been made for them are shown to be valued and appreciated.

Manage calls into the office

> I would prefer to be in a quieter environment because I share the office. Quite often people can burst through the door when I'm in the middle of a phone call. There's three phones in this office, sometimes the other two are ringing out quite loudly while I'm in the middle of a conversation and that can be very distracting, not just for me but for the customer on the other end of the phone.

Interruptions while they are speaking on the telephone make salespeople lose concentration. People would not dream of barging in on a meeting between a salesperson and a customer, particularly if they were in the middle of delicate negotiations, yet it is considered acceptable to stand in front of salespeople on the telephone waving a piece of paper or miming what is wanted. Conversations in the background can be loud enough to be heard by customers. These intrusions make the salesperson lose concentration and often result in having to ask customers to repeat what they have just said. The customer concludes that the salesperson is not interested. Similarly, ringing telephones that go unanswered give out the wrong message to customers who can also hear them, as well as driving telephone salespeople to distraction. Arrange your telephone system in hunt groups that will forward calls to people who are available to answer them.

The following case study illustrates the importance of thinking carefully about the role of the telephone sales team and its impact on customers and the resources of the company.

Girobank case study

Girobank offers its customers an international banking facility which allows them to send money abroad and receive it from abroad. These transactions can be complex, involving documentary bills of exchange and buying currency. The advantage of buying currency is that a company can eliminate any fluctuations in the rate of exchange. It helps to forecast prices with customers and suppliers and so makes budgeting costs easier.

Customers often progress to more complicated transactions once they have experienced the efficiency of the bank in more basic transactions. Therefore the aim of the company is to 'grow' accounts once they have become established and progress them to more complex and profitable transactions. Girobank has discovered that it's only by talking to customers about its financial transactions abroad that it can match its wide range of services to its customers' needs.

Until telephone sales were established these facilities were sold exclusively by the field sales force. Incoming enquiries were dealt with but there was little proactive selling of these products. Customers typically are businesses who have customers or suppliers abroad. There is no segmentation by business size so the team benefits from handling a wide variety of accounts from small business accounts, that is sole proprietors, to international companies. There is no such thing as a 'typical' customer. This adds to the team's expertise and increases team members' confidence when answering customer queries.

This is what the marketing manager has to say about the bank's experience of introducing telephone sales into the international division:

The acquisition process for the international division of Girobank had been under review. We knew that we needed to improve the marketing of the service. The situation was causing concern in a number of areas. Firstly, our existing customers tend to be cash handling customers who are retailers and wholesalers, therefore they are not the market sector which is most likely to be making international transactions. Sales force knowledge and experience in the international sector was, with exceptions, limited as most of their customers did not require this service. Our target market had to be customers who had a certain level of international transactions in order to make it worth their while funding a Girobank account.

The field sales team was naturally primarily focused on retaining and keeping the core product business, the cash handling business. I decided that we needed to increase the acquisition channels and believed that telephone sales would provide the solution. I wanted to prove that telephone selling could be cost-effective and international products and services could be sold to our existing customers provided we targeted them correctly.

Initially reaction in the bank was lukewarm. Various initiatives including telephone selling had been tried before, without much success. Nevertheless I decided that we should try again because attitudes change, markets change, there are different ways of doing things and what might not have been a good idea six months ago could be eminently suitable today.

I think it's worked this time because we have a very good calibre of people doing the job. The team is not only concerned about selling the products and services that we have, they also constantly make suggestions which can improve our service to better fit customer requirements. As a result we have been able to change many processes, procedures and products fairly quickly. When you're selling over the phone customers expect responses to be quick and slick and very controlled. Expectations are much higher. We can have an account open within an hour of having the application approved.

Prospective customers are 'warmed up' by mailshots generated by the marketing department and this stimulates enquiries from interested companies. This can take the form of coupon response requiring further information or direct contact via the telephone.

Telephoning potential customers enables Girobank to establish the type of international transactions the customer is making or receiving, the nature of the business and customers' primary and secondary international requirements. Then the call can develop to telling the customer how Girobank's services match with what they are doing, and how Girobank can improve their existing arrangements.

Quite often the team can close on that first call. Generally customers are very keen to compare price structures. Girobank charges a fixed fee tariff and as some banks tend to charge on a sliding scale, costs can appear very attractive. If the account is not set up on the first call it is usually because the complexity of the transactions demand further investigation either by the bank or by the customer. The aim is to set up a dialogue with customers which allows gentle exploration, and the bank always allows customers time to consider their options. Once an account is opened customers tend to stay loyal to the bank so that it is always with a view to the potential long-term relationship with customers that the bank conducts its sales activities.

Initially there was some concern about how the bank's customers would react to unsolicited telephone calls and the illustration given below by a member of the team points up very well that even the most cynical of customers can be won round if what you have to say interests them.

> I made a cold call to one prospect and when you make a cold call you have to try and grab the prospect's attention with something right away. We had a very low transfer charge that we could offer and I rang up, explained who I was, said the reason I was ringing was because we had this product. I realized that I was getting no reaction at all, so I immediately stopped and said 'Would that be of interest to you?' The answer down the phone was 'Do you know, my dear, I loathe and detest unsolicited phone calls.' There was a long pause and I thought I was going to get an earful of abuse and then he said 'But actually what you have said does interest me.' It has taken about 18 months of continual contact with this particular person mainly because he travels a lot but he has now opened an account. He's got a direct debit with us and two currency accounts and he uses the account a lot. This has all come about by talking him through what it was he needed. So he's got a range of options now which he didn't have before and greatly reduced his bank charges.

After the success, the demonstrable success, of international telephone sales, the company is now looking to put together a large outbound telephone selling unit to sell the product range. Girobank's marketing manager offers this advice:

> Test it. Measure it. Make sure that you have adequate systems and all the angles are covered but don't make a huge investment up front until you are quite sure

that you've got everything refined, you know what you want to say and you know who you are saying it to.

We have done quite a bit of cold-calling. Basically by buying either reference books or reference disks which contain details of our target market. We know that our product or our services are most likely to be appreciated by companies trading with certain parts of the world and so so we spend some time identifying companies that are doing just that and calling them.

You have to be aware of the reputation of your company and take things at the customer's pace, so it can take up to 18 months to actually convert a customer. Be prepared for the long haul but bear in mind that this is a much more cost-effective way of doing it than by having a face-to-face sales relationship because you can keep your customers warm with monthly telephone calls which will pay dividends ... you have to make sure that the sales process actually goes on all the way through the relationship. There's absolutely no point in acquiring a new customer if you are going to lose them within the first six months or 12 months.

It's important that you are very organized about how you keep things like your product information. Is it easily accessible? Is it understandable? Is it valid? Is it updated regularly? The work area needs to be as uncluttered as possible. In my view all you should have is a computer and a telephone/headset, that should be really all that is required. If you don't have your product portfolio and information on your PC then you may need to organize this on your desk.

Finally here is what a successful member of the team has to say about the typical encounters that she has with customers:

I would say try not to sound as if you're reading from a script. I know a lot of people are given a script and I know a lot of people have to stick religiously to that script but I think that will always come over as just somebody reading a script and people like to hear a friendly voice. You should speak to the customer with a friendly attitude, but not over-friendly. I take my lead from the customer, for instance I call and say 'This is Moira Rule from Girobank.' If the customer answers and says 'Yes, it's Mr Smith speaking' I will immediately then start to call him Mr Smith. But if he said 'Oh, hello Moira, it's Jim here, yes what can I do for you' I'll take his lead and call him Jim. So you have to take your lead from the customer. If you go on with a friendly, positive attitude customers generally will respond to that.

Be prepared for rejection. I always try to be positive about it. I think I cope with rejection quite well because there may be a very good reason why I can't sell our products to the customer. For example they might be part of a foreign company that uses a foreign bank. We're not going to win that business but they're not rejecting me, it's the way their business is organized and I can be quite happy with that. I spoke to somebody recently and having had quite a long conversation it was obvious he actually had an excellent arrangement with his own bank. I told him that at present because of the nature of his business we could not offer a better package and he really appreciated it. He said he could tell I was sincere, I hadn't tried to sell him something that he knew was going to be of no use to him and I said 'Well, what would be the point of that' because a banking relationship was something that hopefully is going to go on, it's not about a one-off product. If I had managed to get him to open an account that was unsuitable, he would have eventually closed it and been annoyed about it. This particular prospect/customer said he would contact me in future, as his banking needs changed. We were clear from day one that we wanted to develop good relationships with our customers and I believe that that is exactly what we have done.

Learning points

- Conduct a thorough review of your current sales operation.
- Telesales can provide a further cost-effective customer acquisition channel.
- Segment customer base by size or market.
- You can 'warm up' customers by direct mailing first.
- Cold calls can build up your customer base.
- You can close the sale via the telephone.
- Test market before expanding the telesales operation.
- Take things at the customer's pace.
- Avoid scripts.
- Customers respond to friendly positive attitudes.

Issues to consider

Before you embark on setting up an outbound telephone operation it will help your action planning if you think through the issues that are featured in Figure 1. Use this checklist to guide you through the process.

Tick the box when you have considered the issue.

Making the decision

How will outbound calling enhance your current sales and marketing activities? ❏

What convinced you that outbound calling was appropriate? ❏

What internal resources do you have? ❏

What external resources will you need? ❏

What impact will outbound calling have on the company's other employees? (field sales, administration, etc.) ❏

How will your customers perceive a proactive telephone strategy? ❏

Who will be the key members of the telephone project team? ❏

Recruiting the team

How many telephone sales people will you need? ❏

How many existing employees will be suitable? ❏

What methods will you use to recruit new members of the team? ❏

Have you written a job description? ❏

What criteria will you apply when you recruit? ❏

What will be the selection process? ❏

Will you test for literacy and numeracy? ❏

The induction programme

What will be the length of the induction training? ❏

Figure 1   Making the decision checklist (*continued*)

Who will deliver the training? ❑

What will be the content of the programme? ❑

What contribution can other departments make? ❑

Have you prioritized your training objectives? ❑

Further training

Who will deliver on-the-job training? ❑

Do your trainers/team leaders have relevant experience? ❑

How will you identify training needs? ❑

What 'classroom' training will be needed? ❑

What contribution can product specialists, marketing and colleagues make? ❑

Have you drawn up a schedule for individual and team training? ❑

Managing the team

Have you drawn up personal development plans for the telephone sales manager and the team? ❑

How will the team be structured? ❑

How will you recognize and deal with problems? ❑

What opportunities will the team have for feedback to management? ❑

Will your appraisal process be consistent? ❑

Have you set realistic targets? ❑

Does the team understand your sales objectives? ❑

Figure 1   Making the decision checklist (*continued*)

Is there enough administrative support for the team? ❑

How will you motivate your team? ❑

How will you assess competence? ❑

Do your incentives match the needs of the team? ❑

Have you got the right environment? ❑

How will you recognize excellence? ❑

What steps have you taken to ensure a positive and competitive atmosphere? ❑

Managing team relationships

What information will the team need to communicate to colleagues? ❑

How will the communication process work between the team and the rest of the company? ❑

Will the team be featured in corporate publicity? ❑

What will you use your wall board for? ❑

Have you allowed sufficient time for essential meetings? ❑

What can you do to assist the communication process? ❑

What steps have you taken to avoid conflict where it may occur? ❑

Productivity and technology

What technology will you need? ❑

Who will be involved in developing the system? ❑

Figure 1   Making the decision checklist (*continued*)

How will your customers react to technology? ❑

How will your employees react to technology? ❑

How will you collate information from different systems? ❑

Have you got the sales management information you need, e.g.
key sales ratios? ❑

How will you measure quality? ❑

How will you measure productivity? ❑

Figure 1   Making the decision checklist (*concluded*)

2 How to develop your telephone strategy

Before you initiate outbound calls ask yourself:

1 Who do you want the team to telephone?
2 What type of calls do you want them to make?

Typical outcomes of your telephone strategy might be:

- increased sales;
- closer relationships with customers;
- more repeat business;
- more sales across the range;
- improved sales margins;
- higher conversion rates from quotations to sales;
- problems resolved before you lose customers;
- increased customer knowledge of your products and services; and
- better qualified appointments for your field sales team.

Segment your customer base

It will help you to manage your sales territories and maximize business opportunities if you understand more about the composition of your customer base. Different types of customers will have different needs and concerns. The benefit of doing business with your company can be expressed in different terms to each group of customers depending on their individual circumstances and what is important to them. You can segment in a number of ways, some of which are discussed below.

31

1   Type of business

Your products or services may have wide appeal or be designed to accommodate the needs of a particular market. If they have a broad appeal it may be difficult at first to identify a pattern. You could categorize businesses by whether they are:

- manufacturers;
- service providers, for example hotels, travel agencies;
- distributors, for example electronic components, car components;
- wholesalers, for example domestic supplies, stationery, DIY goods;
- resellers, for example computer hardware and software;
- retailers, chain stores, independent outlets;
- professional services, for example accountants, the legal profession.

Each category of business will have different concerns. You can tailor your sales material to appeal to each segment and personalize the benefits your company can offer to their individual requirements. Mailings can be targeted to specific groups which will increase the response that you get. For example a reseller will be interested in the amount of after-sales support you can offer its customers. Strong after-sales support will encourage it to offer your product in preference to your competitors'. Resellers will be courted by lots of different companies who will all be anxious for the reseller to recommend their product in preference to anyone else's. Although the reseller's recommendations will have to take account of its customer requirements it will also be heavily influenced by how 'safe' its decision will be. If there are any problems the customer will complain to the reseller so it will be concerned about reliability, guarantees and after-sales service. In some cases it will also be interested in promotions that your company may be running to incentivize its sales team. Professionals will be concerned with reputation, status and trustworthiness. Retailers may be concerned with exclusivity to enable them to differentiate themselves from the competition. Of course, all companies will have common concerns but by targeting benefits so that some will have more significance than others for specific audiences, you will ensure that your sales presentation makes a more attractive proposition because it is designed to have particular appeal for your target group.

2   Volume of sales – value of sales

Customers may buy in the following combinations:

1   High volume–low value
2   High value–low volume.

3   Low volume–low value.
4   High volume–high value.

When you have identified their buying patterns you can devise strategies to increase the level of business they do with you or to consolidate the level of business that you already have.

1   High volume–low value: strategy – increase the value of their order.
2   High value–low volume: strategy – increase the number of times they buy.
3   Low volume–low value: strategy – increase the level and value of sales. The customer may be using you as a secondary supplier. Try to get on the 'A' list.
4   High volume–high value: strategy – get close to the customers and consolidate their loyalty.

3   Frequency of sales

When the level of sales is spasmodic this may be due to idiosyncrasies of your customer's business, for example the customer's business may have seasonal peaks and troughs, or it may indicate a rival source of supply. If you can even out the frequency of ordering this will help you forecast sales more accurately because you will not be susceptible to sudden fluctuations in sales.

4   New customers

The first time customers buy from your company is 'the moment of truth'. Does the experience live up to their expectations? New customers need to know that they have made the right decision both for themselves and for their company (or, if a consumer, for their family). A call from your company to discuss their opinion about their experience will reassure customers. This call will hopefully be the beginning of a long-term relationship between your company and the customer. If there are problems they can be resolved. If they are happy the salesperson can ask them when they will be reordering. The timing of the call will depend on what your product or service is. If the customer has taken delivery of a new car, for example, then you should wait until they have had the chance to drive it. A call on the day it is delivered is perfectly acceptable. As a general guideline give customers time to experience the product or service and then call to establish what they think of their decision. The call will also help you to positively reinforce a customer's decision. Remind customers about why they bought. Tell them the benefits again so that they feel they have made the right decision.

5   Existing active customers

These customers are often neglected in the search for new business. Yet they are the backbone of your customer base. Salespeople can become so blasé that they make calls every week that begin 'What have you got for me today?' This is not selling, this is order taking. Salespeople fall into the trap of treating the customer like an old friend who can be taken for granted. The salesperson's needs take precedence over those of the customer: 'I need one more order to reach my target can't you find me *anything*?' Like any other relationship the one between the customer and the salesperson requires work. A lazy approach to customers will result in them becoming dissatisfied or, worse, they will forget what it was about your company that made them purchase from you in the first place. This will make customers susceptible to the courtship of your competitors. A regular programme of 'care' calls should reassure customers that you care about their business and will also keep you up to date with changes in their companies that have the potential to affect yours.

6   Customers who have dual suppliers

Customers may have policies about suppliers that encourage them to use dual suppliers. Using more than one source allows them to 'price check' and helps them to avoid the problems that might occur when a source lets them down either by poor service or by goods not being available when they want them. The problem for your company is that these customers may be asking you for quotations which are expensive and time-consuming to prepare when they are merely using this information to ensure that they are not paying too much to their preferred supplier. Your calls should establish how much business you get compared to your competitors, why the customer uses other suppliers and whether you can offer something that may swing more business in your direction. It is not cost-effective for a company to try to match competitors' prices without some form of commitment from the customer. Increasing this commitment is the main strategy of your calls.

7   Customers who use only one product or service that you offer

These customers may be valued and frequent customers, who for the reasons outlined in point 5 are unaware of the full range of products and services that your company can offer. This occurs when customers have bought from a company for a long time and no one has kept them up to date with changes in your company. If they buy products or services from elsewhere you need to explore their motivations for doing so. Has the customer been advised of the benefits your company has to offer?

8   Infrequent customers

These customers may purchase infrequently because they need reminding to repurchase when their current supplies run out. They will perceive your call as a service rather than a sales call. Customers who need to renew annual agreements for maintenance or insurance fall into this category. Customers might buy products that require replenishing on an *ad hoc* basis. If customers run out of products and stock needs replacing quickly they could become emergency buyers and order from whoever has supplies available. Calls to these customers between purchasing will help to remind them to re-order from you. Customers may not be using your products or services as often as you would like because they do not understand the full benefits of what you are selling. You may need to call to encourage usage and therefore increase buying frequency.

9   Previous (lapsed) customers

Customers stop buying from a company for a variety of reasons. If they have purchased from your company in the past but do not do so now do not be discouraged. They have had a reason to buy in the past and with effort on your part they may buy from you again. Customers can stop buying for a number of reasons:

- A newcomer to the customer's company has an established relationship with suppliers to their old company and wishes to use them in preference to you.
- The customer experienced poor service and so has placed the business elsewhere.
- The customer was attracted to the offers and concessions made by your competitors.
- The customer bought from another supplier because your products or services were less attractive than those of your competitors.

You can overcome customer reservations by talking to your customers about improvements that your company has made to its product or service since they last bought from you. Mistakes do happen and if customers have experienced poor service or faulty goods it will take time to reassure them. Keep trying. Customers are more likely to stop using a company because they do not like the way they have been treated when they have brought a problem to the company's attention than because of what went wrong. Generally customers are willing to forgive. If you can demonstrate what measures you will take to stop them suffering a similar problem they are likely to try you again. Customers want to feel that a company values their business and does not take them for granted.

10   Comparison customers

Potential customers will frequently call a number of companies to compare prices, terms and conditions before they make a decision to purchase. They can be a drain on resources if this results in spending time preparing full costings which result in no sales. Comparison buyers do give you a chance to sell. Someone is going to make a sale and you need to make sure it is you! Instead of sending quotations in the post be there when customers get the information. In other words call them back to give the prices in person. Then you will have the opportunity to answer any questions they may have. If you establish who the competition is it will give you a 'feel' for what the customer is looking for. If you know that the customer is shopping around check the customer is comparing like with like. Price differences may be due to variances in the product or service that is quoted for rather than your products and services being uncompetitive.

Your customer base has enormous potential. Manage it by prioritizing your calls to customers who will yield the highest sales return. Avoid the temptation to 'cherry pick'. Do not spend 80 per cent of your time calling 20 per cent of your customers. Careful forethought and planning will ensure that you call:

- the right customers;
- at the right time;
- about the right products or services.

Outbound telephone activities

The use of the telephone in business is limited only by your imagination. The structure of the outbound sales call is discussed at length in Chapter 5. We will focus here on calls that require a specific approach. These can be categorized as follows:

- Finding new customers: telephone research; prospecting; appointment-making.
- Maximizing sales opportunities: follow-up calls; cross-selling and up-selling.
- Keeping customers: relationship marketing; welcome calls; key account management.
- Developing a contact plan.

Finding new customers

1   *Telephone research*

What do you need to know?

> What never ceases to surprise me is just how much information people will divulge over the phone and how quick it is to build a relationship with them. Customers will tell you pretty much anything about their business, company turnover and their competitors. You can be very frank with them, asking why they won't use you as a business, or why they are using your competitors. Without being confrontational, you can be quite direct. When you phone, you're phoning for professional reasons, yes, you may say 'how are you, it's nice to speak to you again', but then you very quickly get into, 'and the reason for my call is... I'm here to talk to you about...' so I find the telephone far more direct and I've found that customers will tell you an awful lot more.
>
> (Telephone marketing executive)

Using the telephone to conduct desk research will enhance your team's outbound sales activities because it will allow your salespeople to focus specifically on those people who have an interest in or a need for the product or service that you are selling. Even the most sophisticated databases will be redundant if they are not updated regularly. Mailings will be more successful if they are sent to the correct individuals in an organization. Potential and existing customers appreciate the professionalism of a company that spells their names correctly. Research will also ensure that your salespeople contact customers at the appropriate time and this will increase the return on their effort. Telephone research should focus on:

- identifying the decision-makers in a company;
- checking that their company job title is correct;
- understanding where decision-makers fit into an organization;
- learning more about the buying process;
- finding out who influences purchasing decisions;
- gaining information about your competitors and their strengths and weaknesses;
- identifying what the company buys and when it buys it;
- establishing the potential for more business, for example the company may be part of a larger organization;
- discovering when the company will be buying again;
- finding out what quantities / price it purchases.

Your salespeople may need to do some detective work to establish the name and company title of the person they want to talk to. Switchboards can help, but if operators are busy, there is a risk that they will give a name that proves to be incorrect. Some switchboards may have only two operators handling thousands of calls per day so it is not surprising if they want to refer you somewhere else. Company policy not to give the names of company personnel to callers is often invented by harassed operators. Operators should be asked to put the salesperson through to a relevant department where someone will have more time to answer. Frequently people within a department are much more relaxed about giving information and may indeed provide additional useful background information. Alternatively, try another branch or site where the company's 'policy' is more relaxed.

Salespeople should check that the information they have been given is correct before they speak to the contact they have been given.

'I understand that Mr/Mrs ... is responsible for purchasing company cars for your company, is that correct?'

If they think that the person whose name they have been given does not have the authority to purchase or is not as senior in the organization as they would like, they can get around this difficulty by saying:

'Who else, apart from Mr/Mrs ... is involved in this decision?'

Basic research such as address details is best gathered from company personnel who are not decision-makers, for example switchboard operators and receptionists. Whilst this information is essential to the salesperson it is mundane to provide and a busy MD will not appreciate it if salespeople check address details with her. Do not take address details for granted. Companies frequently relocate, sometimes to other parts of the country, whilst still retaining their old telephone numbers. This can lead to problems when appointments are made. Field salespeople can find themselves at a site miles from where the customer is waiting to receive them! A potential source of embarrassment is if the telephone salesperson fails to check whether names apply to a male or female. If a name is unisex, for example Chris, Sam or Pat, check whether the contact is male or female. Asking to speak to Mr Pat Smith gives you no credibility if the person in question is a woman or vice versa. If the contact is female, check how she likes to be addressed, Mrs, Ms or Miss.

Your team can also use the telephone to research existing customers as well as identifying new sources of business. Testing their response to new products or new customer service initiatives could save some expensive mistakes if the reaction is tepid.

Some typical questions your customers might be asked are:

- why they buy your company's products or services;
- what products and services they buy;

- what do they like about your company;
- what do they dislike about your company;
- what changes would they like to see in the future;
- how does your company compare to your competitors – explore strengths and weaknesses;
- are they aware of the full range of products and services that you have to offer;
- how would they respond to a new initiative or process;
- how would they respond to a new product or service.

Customers are willing to participate in surveys, but do be realistic about the amount of time you can reasonably expect a customer to spend helping you develop your business. It is more effective to prioritize the information that you are seeking and begin with the most essential requirements first. Too often, marketing departments get carried away by the amount of information that they think can be gathered in this type of telephone activity and customers are turned off. Some customers may happily spend up to half an hour on the telephone discussing your company but ask yourself, are they 'typical' customers?

It is more productive to spend a short time on the telephone and get answers to vital questions than to spend a long time with customers who are willing to 'chat'.

Follow this call guide for your telephone market research:

The introduction	'Good morning Mr/Mrs ... my name is Fiona Cartwright from Denton and Co.'
Thank customer for taking call	'Thank you for speaking to me Mr/Mrs...'
Check position in company	'I understand that you are ... is that correct?'
If not decision-maker	'Who else apart from you would be involved?'
Once the salesperson is assured that he is speaking to someone who can help he should ask permission to question the customer and state the length of time the call will take	'Mr/Mrs ... I would like to find out more about your company and to confirm that the information I already have is correct. It will take approximately five minutes, are you free to speak to me?
If the customer is too busy, make a telephone appointment	'When would it be more convenient for you to speak, this week or next week?'
Set questions in context	'I would like you to tell me more about how you use our products and services in your company Mr/Mrs...
Ask open questions	'Which of our products and services do you use most?'
Listen for 'free information'	Researcher: 'Where is your HQ?' Customer: 'In the UK? [free information] It's in Leicester.'

> Researcher: 'How many sites do you have other than in the UK?'
> Customer: 'Oh we have 10 other sites around the world.'
> Researcher: 'Really and where are they located?'

[This call has generated information about 11 sites in total rather than just one. Pick up and expand clues offered by the customer.]

At the end of the call   'Thank you for your time, I really appreciate it. Your information will help us to . . .'

Get your team to conduct telephone research of existing customers large and small and all prospective customers. Remember the adage 'Time spent on reconnaissance is seldom wasted.' A telephone salesperson casually tossed some old leads to a new member of the team who wanted some prospecting material: 'There you are. These are old leads so anything that you get will be a bonus. I've given up on them. I don't think that there is any potential there, still they will be good to practice on.' The new member of the team called one of the cast-aside leads and subsequently won a contract worth £50 000 to the company. Unknown to the first salesperson the company was part of a large organization which was about to review its existing supplier. If the seasoned telephone salesperson had done more telephone research then she would have not made this mistake. Keeping up to date with what is going on in prospects' and customers' companies will enable your team to avoid making mistakes like this one.

Case study

A company that sold holidays direct to the public realized that it had a loyal customer base, as was easily identified by the number of repeat bookings it received. It also knew that although it advertised extensively in the national press it was less certain of how its customers were motivated to buy. Many of the customers who rang the company were unable to provide an advertising reference. They were clearly coming from other sources. As so often happens the flow of incoming calls into the company meant that there was not time for the response team to pursue this matter in any detail. Responses from unknown sources went in the 'other' box on the computer screen. Thus the marketing information collated from this source was inaccurate.

The company compiled a list of structured questions designed to elicit both quantitative and qualitative information. The results were both pleasing and surprising. It became clear that most enquiries came via recommendation. Even where customers had used the response mechanisms provided in the press they were usually prompted to do so because friends and relatives had already created a positive impression of the company. In addition, some lovely stories emerged about how its customers felt about the organization. The only significant grumble to emerge from a sample of 100 customers was that voiced by *one* customer who felt it would be preferable to be supplied with four luggage labels instead of the customary three!

Obviously this company was doing a lot of things right but the survey gave it valuable insights about how its customers perceived it. It also caused it to review its marketing activities and devise new strategies to promote the company even more effectively. In addition the sales team was highly motivated knowing that customers liked what the company was doing and the anecdotal stories that emerged gave the team lots of ideas for using these stories on the telephone.

2　Prospecting

Most salespeople find prospecting or cold-calling as it's commonly called the least attractive activity in their busy day and it's often the one that they try to avoid. Somehow there always seems to be things that prevent them from engaging in what is perceived to be a thankless task. The fear of rejection, of upsetting prospects, inhibits people from embarking on what can be the most satisfactory call of all. It is highly rewarding to bring successfully to a conclusion a sale that you have initiated or to make an appointment for a colleague that results in substantial business for your company. Keep the following point in mind:

You have the right to do business

If you are working for a reputable company, and you probably are, your products and services will have been developed to fulfil a need that has been identified by your company. The products and services will be competitively priced because no company sets out to fail. There will be key aspects of your organization that differentiate it from the competition. For all of these reasons prospective customers will be interested in what your salespeople have to say. Prospecting is vital for the growth and success of any company – you may have just the right product or service to help your prospect improve profit or quality in its own business or home. Returns from prospecting are dependent to a great extent on the quality of lead material that you use. There are things you can do to get the best return on your sales team's time:

- Use source material that is likely to yield the best results, for example trade directories, local and national newspapers, trade magazines. Business editorials will familiarize you with what is happening in the marketplace and also give you ideas about suitable prospects for your company.

- Purchase specialist directories which will give you substantial information about prospects, for example a set of directories which gives details of the top 50 000 companies in the UK costs around £450 for the published version or £1500 on CD-ROM.
- Use your own customer database to identify ex-customers. Even if it is some time since they have purchased from your company and they are now 'cold' they had a need at one time so they are potential users of your product or service. All you need to do is to bring them up to date about all the good things that your company has done since they last did business with you!
- Existing customers can provide referrals. If they are satisfied customers they will usually be very happy to do so and will enable your sales team to call prospects with an 'introduction' from your customer, for example 'ZYX Co. have found our products very effective. Mr Jones and Mrs Smith thought that you would find them useful too.'
- 'Warm up' your prospects by writing to them first. Direct mail combined with outbound telephoning is a powerful mix.

Before team members start to telephone make sure that they are unlikely to be disturbed. Prospecting requires a high degree of concentration and distractions or interruptions will prevent them getting into the flow of the calls. Now that you have identified who the team is going to call it is time to think about the content of the call. Use the following guidelines to make your cold calls successful:

1 Decide what you want your salespeople to say. To gain the attention of the prospect they must think of something that will interest the customer. Opening statements can be devised around the following:

   - Changes that have happened in the market.
   - Changes in legislation that might affect the customer's need for your product or service.
   - Changes that have taken place in your own company.
   - Innovations in your product or service.
   - A letter that you have written previously.

2 If the contact is not interested or is not responsible for the purchasing decision, ask your salespeople to discover who else in the organization it would be appropriate to speak to. The call is still worthwhile if they get a further point of contact in the company. Think of prospecting as a continuum. If every call progresses further towards a sale it will have been effective.

3 If the person they wish to speak to is unavailable don't let your salespeople settle for leaving a message, they should ask when the person will

be available and arrange to call back. Secretaries may want to know the purpose of their call, and they should be given sufficient information to establish this, but do not let the call extend to trying to sell to them. Salespeople must always be pleasant and courteous to secretaries, it is their job to prioritize and screen calls. If they give a favourable, confident impression they are more likely to be put through.

4   Salespeople should be well prepared for what they will say to their contact when they get through. They can be caught off guard if they have had difficulty getting through to someone and the contact comes to the telephone unexpectedly. The worst thing that can happen is that they cannot think of a thing to say to them! They should start by explaining the purpose of their call. Prospects do not like to be misled, a direct straightforward approach is best. Saying they wish to conduct research is fine if that is their sole objective. However, do not expect a favourable reaction from the customer if they then try to sell.

5   The team should not worry too much about rejection, if prospects are clearly not interested their time will be better spent talking to people who are. A direct approach will enable them quickly to decide if the call is worth pursuing. The team's time is as valuable as that of their prospects. A call is not worth pursing if:

- prospects indicate reluctance by being unwilling to get involved in the conversation or by talking in general terms that do not allow the call to progress further;
- the prospect has already got a supplier and is contractually bound to it. Call back when the prospect is reviewing its current arrangements. The salesperson will be calling at a time when the prospect is in the market for what the company is offering and therefore will be much more likely to give a favourable response;
- the salesperson is consistently told that the prospect is in a meeting or otherwise engaged, even when the call is pre-arranged. Sometimes you have to take the hint!

Taking the decision not to pursue a call is difficult, a salesperson may be concerned about being perceived as 'giving up', but if prospects are pursued regardless of the signals they are giving, your company will alienate them and their negative reaction will do more harm than good to your company. Every call that is made should leave the receiver of the call with a positive image, both of the salesperson and your company.

6   The telephone is intrusive – you wouldn't barge into someone's office if you could see that they were in a meeting or discussing something with a colleague, so why do it on the phone? It is polite to check that prospects are free to speak to the caller. They will appreciate the courtesy and if they give the go-ahead the salesperson can relax and avoid rushing the call. If a

prospect is too busy to speak to the caller the salesperson should ask when is a more convenient time to call. When the salesperson calls back it will be with the prospect's permission and the conversation is more likely to be successful as the prospect has already indicated a level of interest. Otherwise why did they make the telephone appointment?

3   Appointment-making

Conflicting opinions are held by sales managers when it comes to the issue of making appointments. Some believe that it is more important to see the customer face-to-face and begin the search for a need during the meeting. Others believe that if a need has not been identified the meeting is a waste of time. Whether it's for yourself, a colleague or a member of the field sales team, an appointment is expensive.

Optimize appointments by ensuring that the meeting is:

- with the right person;
- at the right time;
- in the right place.

Customers may be reluctant to meet someone because they:

- are busy;
- do not perceive a need for what your company is offering;
- are worried about being pressured.

Imagine a total stranger wanting to visit you in your home to discuss a business proposition. You would be reluctant, wouldn't you? You might be worried that the caller will be over-persistent or that the product or service is totally irrelevant to you. For a customer to be receptive to the idea of a meeting it is necessary to allay these fears. Whether your customers are fellow business people or consumers they will want to understand the point of the meeting before agreeing to it.

The team may be attempting to make an appointment after your company has sent out direct mail pieces that are designed to stimulate the interest of your customers. Does the following exchange sound familiar?

You: 'Good morning Mr/Mrs ... I sent you a letter regarding the launch
                   of our new service – have you received it?'
Customer: 'No, I haven't.'

Asking a customer if they have received a letter or other information virtually guarantees a negative response. Start calls positively, try the following:

Salesperson:	'Good morning Mrs ... I sent you information regarding the launch of our new service and I would be very interested in your reaction to it. How do you think it meets your current require-ments?'
Customer:	'Well I think ...'

The call starts with the assumption that the customer has received and read the information. Even if she has not it will still stimulate a response that is better than a simple no. Follow up the calls within a week of the mailing going out, otherwise your efforts to 'warm up' the customer will have gone cold.

Close the call by thanking the customer for agreeing to an appointment. Check the arrangements. Ask for a map if necessary. You may want to confirm appointments in writing. A telephone number should be given to the customer so that she can contact the salesperson if it is necessary to do so. Unforeseen circumstances can arise and it is frustrating for a salesperson to turn up to an appointment only to be told that the customer is away ill that week.

Maximizing sales opportunities

1   Follow-up calls

Written quotations that are not followed up are a waste of company resources. Customers and prospects often shop around to benchmark pricing or just to reassure themselves that they are not paying too much to their current supplier. This is fine for the customer but a little wearing for the sales-people who provide the pricing. More effective screening of customers' motives and probing for the opportunity to sell will ensure that your administrative resources are not clogged up. This will also have the further benefit of allowing you to quote customers who are interested more quickly, thus improving the level of service that you are offering them.

Once a quotation has gone out to the customer it must be followed up. Not to do so means that at the crucial moment, that is the moment when the customer is considering whether to purchase, a salesperson is not present to answer any concerns that the customer may have.

Calls should be followed up when:

- the customer has received a quote from the company;
- you know a decision is about to be made.

Before salespeople start a call they must have a copy of the quotation on their desk and any other information that they might need to refer to such as a record of their last call. They should start the call on a positive note. You want the customer to say yes.

'Now that you have received our quotation Mr/Mrs ... how many would you like to order?'

or

'Now that you have had time to consider our discussion last week Mr/Mrs ... I am calling to confirm that you will be going ahead with an order.'

2   Cross-selling and up-selling

There are opportunities for additional business if you explore the full potential of the business that your customers can do with you. You can maximize the return from your account base if you discover where customers source products or services that you are not supplying to them. For example a company that supplied new and recycled toners for printers to its customers quickly discovered opportunities to expand the range it offered. The company had organized itself so that two separate teams sold its products and this meant that opportunities were lost to sell both types of product to its customers. Integrating the sales teams led to increased profits and customer satisfaction. Customers were delighted to source from one company as it cut down their administration costs.

Consider the range of products or services that your company is providing and compare it with what your customers are purchasing from you. There may be opportunities for cross-selling, that is selling different products to the one your customer is buying, or up-selling, that is selling similar products but of a higher specification, better quality or increased volume. Some examples are listed below:

Product	Cross-sell	Up-sell
Office stationery	Desk furniture	Office equipment, e.g. photocopier
Package camping holiday	Travel insurance	A cruise
Camera film	Film processing	Camera
Security cameras	Service contract	Complete security package including security guards
Professional publications	Subscriptions to other publications	CD versions

If you are unsure whether customers may be interested in all the products or services your company has to offer, the best way to find out is to ask them. Every opportunity must be taken to describe what your company has to offer. Questions about what your customers purchase, when and why will enable a salesperson to identify where the company can help them.

Keeping customers

1   Relationship marketing

Companies now recognize that it is more cost-effective to retain customers and increase the volume and value of orders from them than to gain new business. Winning new business is crucial but it makes sense to hold on to customers once you have got them. A company's customer base can become a conveyor belt, dragging customers on at one end and losing them at the other, if there is no attempt to build a relationship with the customer.

Your team can maintain a good rapport with customers by following these guidelines:

- Call customers when it is convenient to them – not to you.
- Use the customer's name in the conversation (not too often, this is irritating and can be perceived as being insincere).
- Listen hard, that is actively, to what customers are telling you.
- Keep customers informed about changes in your business that may affect them.
- Keep up to date with what is happening in your customer's business and in the market in which your customer operates.
- Resolve problems that customers may have had with your company before they affect the goodwill of the customers.
- Demonstrate to customers that you have their interests in mind when you are offering solutions.

Companies that have an established programme of customer care calls can minimize the possibility of customers taking their business elsewhere. Thank your customers for their business and don't take them for granted. If your company launches new, attractive products and services, care calls will prevent loyal customers being left behind. If face-to-face contact is infrequent the care call maintains your relationship with customers and reduces the chances of the competition establishing itself as a preferred supplier.

2   Welcome calls

The first time a customer purchases from your company is a 'moment of truth'. The experience will colour the customer's attitude towards your company for a long time. A welcome call should reinforce the decision and reassure the customer that it has made the right choice when it placed its order with you. Some companies are reluctant to make this kind of call especially if they lack confidence that their customer's experience will be a positive one. Nevertheless even if the customer has experienced some difficulty, perhaps a delivery deadline wasn't met, the welcome call gives you the chance to put things right. Topics you can cover in a welcome call include the following:

- How was it for you?
- Could we have done it better?
- Did we live up to your expectations?
- Was it what you wanted?
- What else can we do for you?
- When you will call again.
- Finish by thanking customers for their business.

3   Key account management

If 80 per cent of your business comes from 20 per cent of your customer base, and according to the Pareto principle it does, then it follows that the loss of one of these 'key' accounts could have a disproportionately adverse effect on your business. Whilst all customers are equal, some are more equal than others. Managing key customers may be solely telephone-based or work in conjunction with field sales. The field sales executive may visit the customer on a regular basis with day-to-day contact conducted via the telephone. Customers are telephone-friendly because they recognize the advantages of using the telephone to speed up the business process. Complex important accounts which were traditionally thought of as exclusively field sales territory are now managed very successfully via the telephone.

Key account management involves three main activities:

1   Ensuring stability of the account.
2   Preventing the competition from winning your customer's business.
3   Maximizing return from the account.

The primary focus of key account management is to develop the relationship between your company and your customer. It involves adopting a partnership approach to business objectives and requires a salesperson to be proactive rather than reactive. Managing accounts successfully is about being aware of the changes that are taking place in the market and in your customer's business. The sales team needs to be up to date with customers' information and this means having a planned programme of calls to their businesses. Silence is not perceived as golden, merely indifference.

Start by identifying those customers that you want to designate as key accounts. Selection of customers depends on a number of factors and these should include the following:

- Customers who purchase high order values.
- Customers whose purchases yield the most profit.
- Customers who have the potential to develop into key accounts.
- Customers who purchase from other suppliers.
- Customers who demand a high level of personal involvement from their suppliers.

Work out your aims and objectives. An aim is a general direction that you wish to pursue (generally long term). Your objectives need to be measurable to allow you to check your progress (can be short and long term). Conducting a SWOT analysis will help to define your aims and objectives. This enables you to identify the strengths and weaknesses of your relationship with the customer, and will help in the formulation of a strategic sales plan. Look at the example below:

Strengths	You have a good relationship with your customer. You offer a good service. The customer likes your product or service, which matches its needs at the present time. Your customer is willing to pay a premium price for what it perceives as a superior product or service.
Weaknesses	You haven't spoken to enough people. You have active competition who can undercut you to win the business. Competitors' products can offer additional features in certain areas compared to your own.
Opportunities	Your customer's business is growing. There are changes taking place in your company that will benefit your customer. Your product or service offers genuine cost benefits for your customer.
Threats	If your main contact leaves the company you could be vulnerable to the competition. Price could become an issue if the customer perceives no difference in quality or features. Your competition could be more flexible than you in terms of price and features.

Once you have conducted the SWOT analysis you can define your aim as:

- to foster closer contact with all key personnel in the company;
- to enhance the perception of the product in the eyes of the customer;
- to resist pressures from intense competitor activity and maintain a profitable relationship with the customer.

A salesperson's objectives might be:

- to identify and contact all decision-makers and influencers in the customer's company;
- to maximize opportunities to demonstrate superior quality and service to the customer;
- to maintain the current pricing structure;
- to explore opportunities to customize the product and service for customers' specific needs.

Use the following checklist to ensure that your salespeople understand what is happening in a customer's business so that they manage the account effectively.

- The responsibilities on both sides are clearly understood.
- They fully understand the structure of the customer's organization.
- All the relevant contacts in the company are known to the salespeople.
- Contacts with the customer are well documented.
- They know how often they need to contact the customer to maintain a profitable relationship.
- They keep relevant people in your company informed of customer issues.
- They allocate sufficient time to develop the account.
- They are aware of the customer's plans for the future.
- They look for win-win solutions.

A primary objective of any telephone key account manager is to prevent the competition getting in. The sales team must know who the competition is both now and in the future, for example who is currently developing new products and services that could pose a threat to the relationship with a customer. Use customers as a source of information about your competition. Find out the competitor's strengths and weaknesses. Imagine a letterbox through which the competition is peering, hoping to be let in by your customer. Even the most faithful of customers can succumb to the charms of the wooer. What are your salespeople doing/offering to keep the competition at bay?

Guidelines for key account managers   If the customer is part of a group, is the competition associated with any sister or subsidiary companies? Could they provide a route into your customer's business? Have a plan to prospect those companies before the competition prospects your customer. Have a customer care programme worked out in detail to ensure total loyalty. This might include special offers, hospitality events, regular updates. Tackle any problem immediately, do not become complacent and treat it without urgency. When you call, check for problems to ensure that none are festering below the surface. Do interesting things for your contacts over and above what is expected – send them information that will help them in their business, for example press or trade magazine articles and research data. Inform customers of the arrangements that you have made for them to be cared for in your absence, for example during holidays, sickness, meetings. Wherever possible make access to you easy for the customer.

Set objectives for account growth and devise a plan that will get you there. Keep asking yourself 'who else', 'what else'. Thinking about what will benefit your customer will help you to suggest new ideas. Have proposals ready for every opportunity: 'if the customer does this I will do that'. Aim to be perceived by your customers as someone who is always trying to help them to be more successful.

Your customer records should include the following:

- Type of business – this will give you an insight into your customers' markets and their customers' concerns.
- Locations – this will provide information about the potential of the account.
- Contact's company title – titles vary from company to company. Check your version is correct. Titles also offer clues about the level of responsibility of your contact .
- Telephone number/extension/direct line/voicemail – always ask for direct numbers so that you can get straight through to your contact.
- The date of your last contact with the customer – dates should be recorded so that you do not leave too long a gap between each call.
- A record of what you discussed and the outcome of the call – records should be accurate so that they are clear to anyone that reads them. Use the account planner in Figure 2 as a template.

Developing a contact plan

It is rare to encounter organizations that delegate the role of 'decision-maker' to one individual. The decision to purchase may involve several people and they may be influenced by others who do not have specific purchasing responsibilities. These 'influencers' will also need to be persuaded that a sales proposal is right for their company. Decision-makers may also have individual priorities and concerns which salespeople need to identify and address if

Company name:	Address:

Delivery address if different: Invoice to:

Other locations:

Contact name	Company title	Telephone number/extension/direct line/voicemail

1 _____

2 _____

3 _____

4 _____

5 _____

Record of customer's spending

Year	Jan.	Feb.	Mar.	April	May	June	Jul.	Aug.	Sept.	Oct.	Nov.	Dec.
1999				£3000	£2000	£250	£1500	£120	£450	—	—	—
2000	£210	£2500	£1600	—	—	£600	£5000	£450	—	£250	—	

Date of contact	Content and outcome of the call

Figure 2   Account planner

their proposal is to be successful. An understanding of the people and the process of purchasing in an organization can be facilitated by the development of a contact plan. The contact plan will help salespeople to direct their proposals to the right people in an appropriate way.

When your team writes an account contact plan team members should ask themselves the following questions:

- Who is my customer?
- What can I do to improve my company's performance?
- What will my company gain from doing so?

Who is the customer? Include directors and functional managers. Think carefully about who will influence the decision. Is the team speaking to enough end-users of your product or service? Their feedback can be a valuable source of information, help and guidance. If the feedback is negative you will need to know about it to develop a strategy to counteract the problem.

What can the company do to improve its performance? Look for opportunities to improve the level of service that your customer gets from your company. You will need to bring negative reaction from your customer to the attention of those responsible in your own organization. This may involve arranging visits from your company personnel to your customer or for key managers from your customer's company to be invited to visit your own premises.

What will my company gain? Any concessions that your salespeople offer your customers must be sustainable without affecting the commercial reality of staying in business. Your company has to make a profit. Concessions should be traded so that negotiations with customers do not result in a win-lose outcome. Always aim for win-win.

There are three approaches to penetrating a complex account:

1 Level – Selling to the most obvious customer opportunities through a very broad coverage of decision-makers at one level, for example calling frequently on a large number of managers with similar responsibilities.
2 Vertical – Selling is concentrated intensely on a narrow range of opportunities. Calls are made to a selected segment of the organization and its line managers, for example distribution, operations, service, etc.
3 Spontaneous – There is no particular plan and calls tend to concentrate on opportunities that are presented by the customer or that are revealed by chance.

The last approach is reactive and unlikely to be cost-effective. If your sales-people allow themselves to be led by your customers, rather than create opportunities to sell, they will have a limited range of opportunities. In addition they will find themselves in a highly competitive situation as other companies will have been invited to respond to the same opportunities.

The best approach is a mixture of level and vertical. Use the level approach to capture information but qualify it realistically. Increase the depth of pene-tration on those opportunities that have been identified to achieve optimum results.

Categorize your sales contacts

1 Decision-makers – people who will have a say in the decision. Their agreement will be necessary before any transaction can take place. In large companies there will be more than one 'decision-maker'.
2 Advocates – people who can influence the decision-makers on your behalf. They will recommend courses of action and are usually referred to by the decision-makers for help and guidance prior to the final decision being taken.
3 Information providers – people who can tell you what you need to know about an organization. They are invaluable for giving an insight into what the organization wants and what will be attractive to it.

Identify the decision-makers' role in their organization

If there is more than one decision-maker in an account it is important to dis-cover who they are. There are usually three tiers of decision-makers:

- Directors .
- Upper and middle management.
- Purchasing managers.

Each group will have different concerns and priorities. It is the salesperson's role to identify what they are and to match the sales approach accordingly. There may be some overlap in the different groups' decision-making criteria but generally they can be expressed as follows.

Directors will be concerned with financial, operational and personnel issues within an organization and how their decisions will affect these three areas of their business. They are responsible for the company's long-term security and how its image is perceived by employees, customers and investors. Financial directors will focus on the return on investment of any money that is allocated to improving the quality of their products and ser-vices. Their eyes will be firmly fixed on the bottom line and they will look for ways to cut costs. To communicate effectively with them you must learn to talk in the language of money. Operational directors will be concerned with reducing the cost of labour, materials and energy without compromising quality. Human resource directors will want to develop their people, improve performance and will be interested in anything that may affect employees' attitudes towards the company.

Upper and middle management will be primarily involved in problem-solving. They will be interested in anything that can help them to resolve everyday difficulties that they encounter. Productivity, sales and improving operations will all be concerns. The problems may be with people, quality control, output, down time or rising costs. They want relief from these problems and tend to think in terms of achieving short-term goals rather than long-term strategy.

Purchasing managers will be at the heart of negotiations on price. They will ask for discounts, bonuses, and extended credit terms in order to get the best deal for their company. They are also likely to be deeply involved in contract specifications and contractual issues. The main task of purchasing managers is to compare the products and services of competing suppliers (or service providers) and to choose the supplier with whom they can negotiate the best terms.

Managers are expensive, busy people. In many cases they do not regard talking to salespeople as part of their job. What do your salespeople need to do to persuade managers when they call them?

- Establish that they have a problem or an opportunity that requires an urgent solution.
- Tell them how they can solve the problem, and describe the effects on their business if they reject the solution.
- Use hard evidence such as statistics, research or testimonials from satisfied customers to back up what they have to say.
- Agree what steps will be taken when the call is finished.

3 Positive telephone selling

Telephone selling is not a cheap alternative to selling face-to-face. If the team is to succeed the whole company and all of its employees must be willing to make the changes necessary to allow the team to operate effectively. If the team needs to send out quotations or information to customers then the administrative processes in your company must accommodate this. Positive telephone selling requires the following:

- Sufficient resources.
- Enough qualified leads and accounts to call.
- Investment in training.
- Efficient communications both in-house and externally.
- Commitment from the top down.
- Time to develop and consolidate.

If switching to outbound calls is a radical departure from your normal communication with your customers, you may feel a little apprehensive. What is your customers' reaction likely to be? The telephone is intrusive and if the timing of the call is off it is possible that you could annoy or irritate customers. It is a simple matter to arrange to call your customers at a time convenient to them. Make telephone appointments, customers will appreciate your courtesy.

Telephone selling from the customer's point of view

If you are calling existing customers they will perceive the call to be part of the service that you offer. If there have been changes in your company that will affect your customers, it is helpful to let them know about them. They may have questions that they wish to put to you. If there has been an increase in your product range then the customer will want to be informed. In other words, your call will be perceived as a *service*, not an intrusion. This is equally true of cold calls to prospective customers. If your product or service is capable of improving the prospects' current arrangements, then you will stimulate their interest. Target your calls to those who will have an interest in what you are selling. Lack of targeting leads to a 'spray gun' approach, that is make lots of calls and hope that something sticks.

It is true that customers are irritated by unprofessional telephone selling but this is true of any profession where incompetence is encountered. Customers demand competence from all service providers, why should telephone selling be the exception? To avoid some of the pitfalls that incompetent salespeople may bring upon themselves you should be aware of what annoys customers most. Here are common criticisms of incompetent telephone salespeople:

- They don't listen.
- They talk too quickly making it difficult for the customer to follow.
- They are unknowledgeable.
- They are unsure of company procedures, policy, etc.
- They are more concerned with getting their message across than with finding out just how suitable their product or service is for the customer.
- They are over-familiar.

All of these criticisms can be rectified if you develop effective communications skills. If your team's confidence is undermined by lack of knowledge about your company, fill in the gaps as part of a formal training programme and encourage them to use their own initiative to build up their expertise. Customers welcome calls from telephone salespeople who:

- target their call activity to those who are likely to be interested in the proposition;
- explain the purpose of their call;
- establish that their timing is convenient for the customer;
- ask 'sensible' questions;
- offer clear, lucid descriptions;
- treat the customer as an individual not just another number to call;
- are interested in the outcome of the call;
- are enthusiastic without being gushing; and
- take no for an answer.

What is 'positive telephone selling'?

Positive telephone selling refers not only to the commitment of individuals, that is the telephone salespeople involved, but also the management team and everyone in the company who could be considered to have an impact on the team's performance. If a company is half-hearted in its attempts to sell via telephone the team will fail. There must be planned effort that reflects commitment, through investment in personnel and resources, to increase the level of business that is done on the telephone. The telephone sales team can affect the outcome of the venture by the attitude of the salespeople and the level of skills that they apply to the role. If team members are not convinced that the company has a genuine contribution to make to the improvement of a customer's products or services then they have little hope of persuading customers to buy. When a company embarks upon telephone selling the key to the success of the venture is to support the sales team and to make available the necessary resources to achieve success. If a company sees telephone selling as a route to cutting costs and as second best to field sales activities then problems will occur. Take positive action to introduce effective telephone selling in the following ways.

The role of management

1 Train the team adequately before launching the department

Such training goes beyond the content of an induction course. Not only is it necessary to induct the team in the process of how the company conducts its business, it is necessary to enhance team members' sales skills and increase their knowledge of the product. Even if the team is responsible for only one part of the sales process, for example appointment-making, the first encounter with prospective and existing customers will be diminished if the team lacks credibility to discuss customer concerns because team members don't know enough about the business. First impressions will be the only impression that a customer has of the company if the call doesn't progress from there. That first impression must be a positive one. Some sales managers believe that if an appointment-making call goes into too much depth the customer may not wish to see someone face-to-face, and therefore it is unproductive for an appointment-making team to have 'too much knowledge'. This could be counteracted by the response 'a little knowledge is a dangerous thing'.

2 Update training regularly and provide on-the-job coaching

Training must be continuous and relevant. The training manual should be reviewed regularly and reflect current practice of the team. Stand-alone train-ing, especially if conducted in a classroom environment, will not be effective unless supplemented by on-the-job coaching. Where possible, listen to and use live call examples in your coaching sessions. Coaching will also provide the opportunity to reinforce training messages. It is a mistake to assume that because someone knows the theory, they practise it. Only constant practice will improve sales skills, not spasmodic concentrated sales training. Even well-established successful teams will benefit from coaching that develops their skills. You can also incorporate the team's own solutions to sales situa-tions into your training material. Teams appreciate real life scenarios which they can relate to, rather than off-the-shelf material.

The role of the telephone sales team

1   Be powerful advocates for the company

What makes you so special? Why should I do business with you? These are the questions that all telephone salespeople should be able to answer imme-diately. Did you? If salespeople cannot find the appropriate words to per-suade a customer that the company is a good company to do business with, then who can?

2   Build positive relationships with customers

Take your time. Sales calls last a matter of minutes not hours, and telephone selling can fail to make the right impression on a customer because the call is hurried. In an effort to squeeze everything in the salesperson sounds panicky, not relaxed and authoritative. This can lead to one-sided conversa-tions with the telephone salesperson doing all the talking. When these calls are followed up the customer is unavailable. No one wants to be talked at. To develop a rapport with the customer which can build into a long lasting rela-tionship, it is wise to diagnose the illness before attempting to offer the cure. A sale may take many telephone calls to complete and therefore it is more realistic to accept that the first call will be one where you are seeking to estab-lish whether your product or service is relevant to the customer. To find out you need to encourage the customer to do the talking and not hog the conver-sation yourself.

3   Communicate customer opinion to relevant departments and people

Feedback from customers is likely to fall into three areas:

- Positive feedback about colleagues.

- Positive comments about your product or service.
- Negative comments about the product or service.

A telephone sales team is likely to receive valuable feedback from customers. All information that is likely to influence the actions of colleagues and other departments should be communicated back to individuals and managers. If someone has done something well and the customer has praised them, positive feedback from the team will be appreciated by colleagues. It will also reinforce their commitment to provide good service because they will know that it is valued. Similarly, marketing and product managers will need to know what customers are demanding from the company and whether your company is meeting customer expectations. Customers are likely to be more honest about what they think of your company when they communicate on the telephone than in a face-to-face meeting. People are more forthright on the telephone. Think of occasions when you have complained via the telephone and situations where you have complained in person. Compared with a face-to-face meeting people are so much braver on the telephone! If you receive complaints from customers give others a chance to put things right.

4 Focus on the company's strengths not its weaknesses

Your company will inevitably be more competitive in some areas than others. Customers may be more aware of the negative aspects of your company than the positive ones. It is easier to remember the bad things than the good. So, if a customer is telling you about your company's weaknesses counteract this with the good things that you know your company can do. Even if your product or service is difficult to differentiate from your competitors' there is always a unique factor that cannot be provided elsewhere – you!

5 Look for sales opportunities

Don't be content just to take orders from regular customers. Analyse your sales records to understand buying patterns. Does demand for certain products come from a particular profile of customer and do all your customers who fit this profile know about the product? Customers may be purchasing from other suppliers with or without your knowledge. Opportunities can present themselves in a number of ways:

- To increase volume:
    - sell other products or services to the customer;
    - sell to different departments or sites in the customer's organization that do not buy from you now;

- keep up to date with what is happening in your customer's company. Changes in your customer's company could mean increased sales opportunities for you.

- To increase profit:
  - negotiate the best price for your company;
  - avoid using discounts to win business, sell the benefits of your product or service.

6   Use initiative

The tension that sometimes exists between a telephone sales team and the sales manager can be summarized thus:

The manager doesn't know what they are doing (your view).
The team doesn't know what it's doing (the manager's view).

Problems often occur through lack of communication; ironic isn't it? If a team has a problem nothing will happen if you do not tell anyone about it. Managers always welcome constructive ideas for improvement. Listening to other people's ideas and then implementing them is how they got promoted in the first place. So if you want something to change it is more productive to come up with a proposal for implementing that change than to moan about the status quo. Look for solutions and ideas that you can initiate rather than waiting for others to do it for you.

7   Be ready to accept responsibility

Achievable targets are not a myth. If the team is behind target look for the reasons rather than finding excuses. The achievement of target is the team's responsibility. The team should also accept responsibility for:

- its productivity;
- the discounts that are given to customers; and
- the concessions the team negotiates with customers.

8   Take measures to improve your knowledge and skills

Some telephone salespeople take the view that all their training and development must take place between the hours of 9a.m. and 5p.m. – 'If I don't get paid for it I'm not doing it.' If the team works in an environment where there isn't time during the course of the normal working day to improve skills and knowledge then, rather than do nothing, look for ways to compromise.

After hours training can be motivational and fun. If it increases success then monetary reward will follow. Use your team's experience to help to develop the skills of newcomers. Listen to each other on the telephone and be prepared to give each other feedback. Include training in team meetings.

9 Take in the big picture

A company is the sum of its parts. Obvious, yes, but easily forgotten in the intense atmosphere of the telephone sales room. Other departments are there to support you and your customers. Your internal relationships with colleagues should be positive. You can take the following steps to foster good relationships:

- Visit other departments to see at first hand what they do and how they do it.
- Ask the question 'What can we do to make your job easier?'
- If there are company 'policies' that you don't understand find out more about why they exist and their purpose. Seeing a situation from a different perspective will help you to explain your company's position to your customers.
- Invite colleagues to your team meetings and attend theirs.
- If you have a problem with another department do something about it. Try to resolve it directly with the people involved before you step up the pressure for change via your manager.

Positive telephone selling is all about focusing on what you and your company does well. It is about what you can do not what you can't do. The perfect company would have the world beating a path to its door. Other companies, like yours, do some things better than others. Strive for improvement and recognize when you have failed, put it right if you can and move on. Advocates do not engage in running down their own organizations, they recognize and communicate what a company has to offer. What makes you so special? Why should I do business with you?

The case study below demonstrates the importance of consolidating the relationship you already have with your customers by using the telephone to maintain contact with them. It also highlights the importance of recognizing the achievements of your team and how management is assessing and evolving processes constantly.

BT case study

BT has launched the largest programme of outbound telephone marketing in the UK. The programme is at the heart of its strategy to retain residential customers. Competition from cable companies and other telecom businesses has demanded proactive intervention to prevent BT's customer base from being eroded. Outbound telephone selling has received a massive endorsement from the company and its belief is underwritten by an enormous financial investment, currently amounting to some £100 million in call centres around the UK, and the creation of 3000 jobs.

Therese Eltringham is call centre manager of the flagship site in Warrington which employs some 1900 people:

We use the phone for contacting our existing customers with the overall objective of increasing loyalty and consolidating our relationship with our customers. We establish that they are happy with our service and we offer them products and services that will improve what they have already. The loyalty programme has protected the customer base. Given the scale of the investment, each call centre costs approximately £20 million. It was a Board level decision to go ahead with the telemarketing and it indicates the commitment to the project at senior management level.

At this site we've got a management structure of around 150 people and a support structure of about the same amount, so of the 1900 people on site we've got about 300 who aren't actually on the phone. The call centre is open from 9.00 in the morning until 9.00 at night with an hour break between 3.00 and 4.00. The morning shift is a staggered start from 9 o'clock, finishing at 2.30 p.m. The management for that shift will come in at 7.00 in the morning and work until about 3.30 in the afternoon. There's an overlap because the managers from the afternoon shift arrive at 1 o'clock and we then start phoning at 4 o'clock until 9.00 p.m.

We use all sorts of different advertising methods, including TV, cable TV, press ads, and boardings to recruit. We also talk to school leavers at all the local schools and local universities. We have an open day or evening where they come along and see the call centre. If they are interested they will go through quite an intensive assessment process. They'll have verbal and numerical tests and an in-depth interview where we will go through exactly what the job is. We explain that it's a customer retention role and that whilst there's an element of customer service it's sales as well. People tend to either have customer service experience or sales experience and we explain that we want a blend of both.

New entrants go through a two-week training programme which covers everything from the environment within which we work, which is regulatory, and the importance of the customer. We describe the ethos of the company, how we manage our people, the ways in which we speak to customers, the ways in which we treat each other so that the values of the company are known and the behaviour of our employees supports those values. Next comes full product and systems training in a classroom environment. There is constant assessment and it is a pass or fail course. Once they have actually passed through the first two weeks they then enter what we call graduation day. This means that they are still in a classroom environment, they don't go out to a sales team immediately but they now have a sales manager as well as a trainer with them to enhance their sales skills. After a probationary period they are appointed to a permanent team and should be achieving all of their targets.

We're heavily reliant on technology because it's a large-scale call centre and the technology underpins everything we do. We've got fully blended inbound and outbound technology, predictive diallers. We can tape calls and play them back remotely which gives us the ability to monitor second-by-second real time the performance of our teams and the performance of our centre. We use random monitoring to maintain quality and ensure that our teams are adhering to, not just the flavour, but the words of the script.

The structure of the script explains the purpose of the call, how long we're going to take and asks for permission to continue with the call. Once that is granted we check some customer details then move to talking about what products and services we have to offer and why they would be of benefit to the customer. At the end of the sales call we recap all of the information that has been given to the customer. We confirm what has been agreed, e.g. costs and availability, and everything is confirmed in writing so that the customer is absolutely clear about everything that has been discussed.

Now that we've established the use of the scripts, we are confident that we can move some of our people to call guides. We are in the process of testing that and the guide will be based on quality benchmarks. The advantage of going from a script to call guides, which would be a bulleted list of the key messages, is that it can be mundane repeating the script word for word. We want to allow them to project a little bit more personality and achieve more interaction with the customer. As long as the people are fully trained it's of mutual benefit to customer and advisor.

Within the company there is a huge amount of support for what we are doing. We are trying new things out and it's new to the business but because there is overall support for the objectives and the way in which we do things, then people do get recognized for doing a good job. So we are not the poor cousins of the company by any stretch of the imagination, we're more of a flagship.

Learning points

- You can use the telephone to increase loyalty and consolidate your relationship with customers and protect your customer base.
- Commitment at senior management level will help to secure the appropriate investment.
- A ratio of one manager (includes team leaders) per 10.6 employees with a similar ratio for sales support. Note that the level of sales support will be determined by the complexity of the product or service that you are selling. If complex written quotations are required this figure may be higher.
- If you are selling at times outside 'normal' working hours a mix of full and part time staff will work.
- Invite potential recruits into the workplace so that they get a full picture of what the job is all about.
- Assess for literacy and numeracy.
- You can recruit candidates from either a customer service or sales background. It is possible to devise a training programme that will enable employees to blend both skills to achieve the company's objectives.

- Explain the company's values. If your salespeople are going to communicate the right message they need to know what it is.
- Include product and systems training as well as sales skills in your training programme.
- Don't throw new recruits in at the deep end. Ensure that they have the appropriate level of support until they have achieved the level of competence that you desire.
- Use statistics generated by the telephone system to measure productivity and random monitoring to check quality.
- If the customer makes a buying decision confirm what has been agreed in writing so that there are no misunderstandings.
- Scripts can help new recruits to build their confidence and ensure consistency but it is possible to develop their skills further by introducing call guides which give the caller some flexibility during the call.
- Recognize excellence and achievement.

The case study below demonstrates how a company's management team can support their internal sales department.

Dr Solomon's Software case study

Dr Solomon's mission statement is:

> To be the global leader in anti-virus technology, products and markets. Strengthen and grow from our success in anti-virus in the UK and Northern Europe. Provide the highest quality products and services to our customers world-wide.

Dr Solomon's Software, the world leader in computer virus detection, identification and disinfection, is an international company founded in 1984. The company is recognized for its technically superior anti-virus solution, Dr Solomon's Anti-Virus Toolkit, a cross platform set of products with an installed base exceeding 10 million world-wide and which detects more than 17000 currently known viruses.

Dr Solomon's Software employs more than 500 staff world-wide and has offices in Burlington, MA and Raleigh, NC, USA; Aylesbury, UK; Hamburg, Nuremberg and Munich, Germany; Basel, Switzerland; and Melbourne and Sydney in Australia. In addition, Dr Solomon's products are distributed by 58 international partners in over 100 countries. World-wide bookings for the year ended 31 May 1997 exceeded £45 million ($72 million).

Dr Solomon's route to market comprises a number of channels, either directly to the end-user or via Dr Solomon's authorized corporate resellers and authorized distributors and retailers.

The internal sales department specializes in direct telephone selling to small and medium-sized businesses who have between 50 and 1000 PCs. The revenue from this team has grown by over 30 per cent every year since its inception. Now in its fourth year as a business unit it contributes over 24 per cent of total revenue to the UK business. The internal sales team is 15 strong and is set to grow further in the next financial year. The team is both reactive and proactive.

The team acts as the first point of contact for many prospective and existing customers and therefore has a high volume of inbound telephone traffic. This is managed by an ACD (Automated Call Distributor) system which ensures that customers get through to the right person first time. The ACD also enables Dr Solomon's to manage sales and marketing resources by providing statistical information such as volume of calls and source of enquiry.

Proactive telephone selling takes the form of prospecting and account management. The renewals team maintains and builds relations with existing customers by contacting existing clients. This is achieved by keeping in close contact with customers, enquiring on progress, discussing outstanding issues and matching their needs with new products or services as they become available. This service-oriented sales method has proved to be invaluable in satisfying and retaining customers as well as being able to achieve (and exceed) sales targets. Customer retention rate is now over 95 per cent and the revenue from each customer increases by approximately 30 per cent at the time of the licence renewal.

The sales and marketing tracking system enables any person within the team to deal with a customer and therefore Dr Solomon's can offer a seamless service to both potential clients and existing customers. Of course, the database is only as good as the information it holds and therefore a checking system has been implemented to ensure that the quality of information entered into the database is of a high standard.

Working with other sales departments is the key to a successful sales strategy. As internal sales is often the first point of contact it is important for the team to be trained to qualify leads properly, and to have a good understanding of how the other departments operate in order to offer good customer service and get answers quickly.

At structured weekly meetings the team is informed of changes to products or working practices and is able to question a relevant guest presenter. Moreover, a buddy system has been developed where an internal sales executive will be linked with a corporate account manager, thus enabling Dr Solomon's to maximize the potential within an existing account.

The new business team follows up pre-qualified leads. It is essential that these potential customers receive a fast and efficient service and so the team leader ensures that all leads are followed up within pre-specified timescales. Part of the new business team's activities is to develop new opportunities through cold-calling. Each member of staff is also given responsibility to develop and penetrate a particular market sector.

Telephone marketing is undertaken by an outside agency. In order to ensure a steady flow of quality leads the relationship is managed by a project leader. Any agency personnel working on the account are given an introduction to the company and spend one or two days working within Dr Solomon's. They leave with a good understanding of the culture of the company and can then speak to potential clients as if they were part of the Dr Solomon's team.

Systems are a major part of any telephone sales or telephone marketing environment and Dr Solomon's relies heavily on set procedures and internal database systems. The procedures enable the telephone sales team to work efficiently in order to provide excellent customer service and therefore maximize revenue.

The knowledge and skills acquired within the telephone sales environment should be utilized effectively by developing a career path either within the department or elsewhere in the company. As part of that development process Dr Solomon's offers both structured training courses and on-the-job training and is also supportive of staff in achieving a national vocational qualification (NVQ) in telephone sales.

Learning points

- Sales channels comprise different customer bases from end-users to distributors and resellers. Therefore the sales activity was customized to the needs of each segment.
- In the four years since its inception the internal sales team has achieved 30 per cent growth year on year.
- ACD supports the effective distribution of calls and allows the company to manage its resources more efficiently.
- Proactive telephone selling focuses on prospecting qualified leads and account management.
- Close contact with customers improved the renewal rate. There was a direct business benefit in resolving customer concerns before they disaffected the customer. Not only does the company achieve 95 per cent retention but the point of renewal provides it with the opportunity to increase revenue from a customer by as much as 30 per cent.
- Timescales for following up pre-qualified leads are pre-specified so that return is maximized.
- Cold-calling is used to grow the customer base. Each telephone salesperson is given responsibility to define and develop market opportunities.

- Where an external agency is used it is beneficial to allow agency personnel the opportunity to absorb the company culture. This ensures a consistent corporate message to prospective customers.
- The database is quality checked to ensure reliable information is available to the sales teams.
- Weekly meetings are structured. Guest presenters add value to the meeting by providing information to the team and cementing internal relationships.
- Use a 'buddy' system. It will help to synchronize the efforts of the internal and external sales teams.
- Look for ways to provide a career path for ambitious high achievers.

(You can develop the skills of your team and improve their morale by providing them with the opportunity to gain nationally recognized qualifications. This will benefit both the individual and the company. Readers who would like more information about NVQs can contact The Sales Qualification Board at The Brackens, London Road, Ascot, Berkshire SL5 8BJ, Tel. 0171 872 6937.)

4 Essential skills to enhance telephone effectiveness

To communicate successfully over the telephone your team will have to demonstrate confidence and competence. Because the customer has no visual clues communicating effectively over the telephone is limited if appropriate attention to development of verbal interpersonal skills is not given. Use the material in this chapter to develop training modules that will allow your salespeople to understand the impact of ill-considered communication on customers. People don't always say what they mean and people don't always mean what they say, therefore we have to listen for clues and analyse not only the content of what is said, but context and tone.

Everyone at some time has formed an impression of a company or an organization purely on the basis of telephone contact. This impression may be positive or negative and an individual speaks for the whole organization when he or she converses with customers. Help your telephone salespeople to understand that just as they form powerful images and impressions of the customers that they speak to, so customers form opinions of them. Time on the telephone is limited so make every word count.

Confidence breeds confidence

A confident manner will enhance the probability of making a favourable first impression on a customer. If you are confident a customer will respond to your approach more positively. Most calls are quickly terminated by customers when they feel that their time is being wasted or that the caller isn't really interested in the outcome of the call. Look at the following phrases and consider their ability to instil confidence in the customer about the competence of the caller.

'I wonder if you would spare me a few moments of your time?'
(salesperson is projecting: 'Which is so much more valuable than mine.')
(customer is thinking: 'No, why should I?')

'Hello Mr/Mrs ... it's only me.'
(salesperson is projecting: 'I'm unimportant.')
(customer is thinking: 'Oh no, not again.')

'I'm sorry to bother you.'
(salesperson is projecting: 'I can't think of a single reason why you would want to talk to me.')
(customer is thinking: 'You are bothering me.')

Confident callers are positive about the benefits to the customer of accepting a call from them. A professional, competent and friendly approach is rarely rejected. Customers don't reject calls or proposals without a good reason. Usually it's because they have no confidence in the person who is contacting them. If you are confident, your customers will be confident.

Using positive language

Using positive language means keeping what you say clear, simple and free from jargon. It will help you to create a rapport with your customers if you match their pace and vocabulary. The words that you use can make a great deal of difference to how customers react to your ideas or suggestions. Talk about what you can do, not what you can't do. Choose words that accentuate the positive aspects of your proposal or suggestion and avoid negatives.

Words that have a positive connotation will reassure your customers and help them to recognize that they are doing the right thing.

Negative words	Positive words
Objection, hesitation, rejection, reluctance	Concern
Sell, retail, canvass	Transaction
Buy, purchase, procure	Own, secure
Cost, price, amount, expense	Investment
Deal, obligation, contract, paperwork	Agreement
Problem, doubt, issue	Question, ask
Pitch, present	Demonstrate, show
Signature, endorse, confirm	Approve
Feature, property, trait, characteristic	Virtue
Need, want, obligation, pre-requisite	Requirement

Positive framing

By couching your response to customers in a positive frame you convey what you will do (positive) not what you won't or can't do (negative).

Negative	Positive
'I don't know.'	'I will find out.'
'We don't do that.'	'What we can do is . . .'
'It's company policy.'	'We do this because . . .'
'I can't have this ready until next week.'	'I will have this ready for you next week.'
'I can't do that until the new computer system is installed.'	'I can do that when the new computer is installed.'
'We are out of stock.'	'Our stock will arrive on . . .'
'I don't know, I'm new here.'	'I will check with my colleague.'
'You will have to complete these forms.'	'When you have completed the forms we can . . .'
'I will need some details to do a credit check.'	'I can establish a credit line for you once I have a few details from you.'

Here are some useful positive phrases that will help you to convey a positive impression to your customers:

Of course I can	That's interesting, please tell me more about that
I would be delighted to	
I can help you with that	Thank you for your comments
	You have made a good decision

Slang and lazy phrases

When you communicate with your customers misunderstandings can occur because you have a level of knowledge about your company or the market that the customer may not have. Using abbreviations for departments or services is a typical example.

Caller: 'Well Mr/Mrs . . . I'll inform our CSS department and they will send you a copy of our F14 leaflet which will explain how to install the 7890 model using dual systems.'

Customer: 'Eh?'

Lazy phrasing is indicative of not really 'tuning in' to the call. Your mind is on other (more important?) things. Look at the examples below, do any of them sound familiar?

'Cheers'	'Bear with me'
'I'm not sure'	'Off the top of my head'
'Roughly'	'He's no longer with us'
'Hi'	'Okey-dokey'
'Just a minute'	'It's June calling'
'I've no idea'	'CSS dept, can I help you?'
'All I can do is . . .'	'OK mate'

'Your order should hopefully be ready by next week sometime'
'Hold on a sec.'

'I'll see to that as soon as I can'
'Give me a moment'

Express yourself positively by being specific and using professional terminology. Although some may argue that a cheerful informal approach is acceptable, particularly if your customers are casual in their own speech, it does have the disadvantage that when the going gets tough you may lose credibility in the eyes of the customer. Customers may want to speak to someone who has more status in the company because they feel that you do not have enough authority to negotiate for example.

Customer: 'I want to speak to Jimmy Collins please.'
Employee: 'That's me mate, what can I do for you?'
Customer: 'I've received a quotation from you and I think the price is too high. What discount can you give me?'
Employee: 'Sorry mate, that's the best I can do.'
Customer: 'Can I speak to someone in charge? I want to negotiate a better price.'
Employee: 'Sorry, I'm new here. Just a sec. [*pause*] Well, I'm not sure, but off the top of my head I think you should speak to Mrs Evans in our CSS department. Hold on ... sorry, there's no reply, what do you want to do?'
Customer: 'I'll call back.'
Employee: 'Cheers ... er ... OK then.'

The power of your voice to create images

When you listen to the radio you imagine the pictures it creates in your mind. A similar process takes place on the telephone. Think of people that you have spoken to but never met. Although you have only their voices to rely on, nevertheless you 'picture' what they look like. You also draw conclusions about what sort of people they are, for example 'nice' or 'difficult'. Often when you do meet customers face-to-face you are surprised, pleasantly or unpleasantly, at the reality compared to your mental image.

How do customers picture you?

Your voice betrays your emotions and reveals what you really think. It isn't enough to say the right words, you must project the right attitude. You can say 'good morning' in a warm friendly tone or inject the words with sarcasm or indifference. Try it and see. A monotonous voice tone can quickly lead to boredom. Customers will 'switch off' from what you are saying. 'Fabulous' does not sound fabulous when you say it in a bored and dull monotonous voice. However, too much change in tone can lead to dramatic delivery which sounds theatrical and false (gushing).

The way that you use your voice tone and inflection is important. Consider the following sentence:

'What can I do to help you?'

Now say it in a voice tone that expresses a different attitude each time:

Angry	Confident
Upset	Friendly
Concerned	Efficient

Now say the same sentence with a different inflection on the words:

'**What** can I do to help you?'	'What can I **do** to help you?'
'What **can** I do to help you?'	'What can I do to **help** you?'
'What can **I** do to help you?'	'What can I do to help **you**?'

On the phone, you have to rely on your voice and manner to make an impression. Here are some suggestions to help you.

1   Speak at a slightly slower rate than usual

If you speak too quickly it makes it easier to be misunderstood and mistrusted. Conversely, speaking too slowly can make the customer impatient or irritated. People who wear glasses frequently remark that they 'hear less well' without their glasses. This is because we communicate using body language as well as verbally. It is more difficult to follow a conversation without visual clues. To check this ask a colleague to turn his or her back to you and read a passage from a book. You will find that following what is said is harder to do than if the person were speaking to you face-to-face. To enable customers to follow what you are saying, compensate for lack of visual clues by consciously slowing your rate of speech to give your customer time to assimilate what you have said. If customers have to ask you to repeat what you have said this usually indicates that you need to slow down.

2   Smile. Use a warm tone of voice

Though a smile cannot be seen, it does change the tone of your voice. Try to sound pleasant, efficient and, perhaps most important, interested and enthusiastic about the conversation. Enthusiasm is contagious. A telephone marketing manager of a national financial services company insisted that her salespeople sat with mirrors in front of them so that they could do a 'face check'. The aim was to ensure that they were aware of their facial expressions when they spoke to customers. You can tell if someone is smiling when they speak to you on the telephone. Think of conversations that you have had with friends or colleagues on the telephone when you have said 'What's the matter?' to their first greeting. What gives away their mood is their tone of voice. It is hard to inject a warm tone of voice if you are not smiling. Of course, if the situation calls for gravity smiling is not appropriate, so match your mood to that of your customer.

3   Use emphasis to make your point

You can emphasize the parts of the communication that are important to the listener or emphasize for clarity. 'Signpost' the important content of the conversation by using phrases such as:

'Here's a really interesting fact . . .'
'This is important . . .'
'You will particularly like this . . .'
'This next bit is especially relevant to you . . .'

4   Ensure clarity

Make sure you are heard correctly, especially names, numbers, etc. It is easy to confuse S's and F's or T's and G's for instance, or for the customer to hear 15 per cent instead of 50 per cent.

5   Be concise

Use short sentences with a logical sequence and discuss one thing at a time. Watch out for and avoid the wordiness that creeps in when we need time to think, for example 'at this moment in time' (now), 'along the lines of' (like).

6   Use gestures

Your style will come across differently depending on your posture. For example there are certain kinds of call that you can do better standing up rather than sitting down – when you feel a lack of confidence or wish to emphasize a particular point. If your posture is too relaxed your voice might lack authority and clarity. If you are slouched your voice will reflect this. It is not unusual to see salespeople emphasizing their conversation with hand gestures, although customers cannot see these they do serve to enhance communication because your enthusiasm for a subject will be transmitted to the customer.

7 Be natural

Be yourself. Avoid adopting a separate, contrived, telephone personality. A 'telephone voice' will convey insincerity. Do not behave or project yourself differently from how you would if you were speaking to friends and colleagues.

8 Obtain input from your customer

Talk *with* customers not at them. As a first step to encourage response, form a picture of your customer and use this to remove the feeling of talking to a disembodied voice.

Other aspects of tone and inflection that will influence your customer's perception of you are:

- Loudness – too loud and you will turn customers off. They will find it difficult to concentrate on what you are saying. Customers will feel that you are shouting at them.
- Softness – if customers have to strain to hear what you are saying they will soon lose their ability to concentrate on the content of your message.
- Pitch – if you tend to allow your voice to rise at the end of sentences customers may feel that you are asking questions rather than stating facts.
- Articulation – if you mumble your words customers may misunderstand what you are saying. If you are over-precise in your articulation they may feel patronized.
- Accent – you *can* make an accent work for you as it can differentiate you from the crowd. Accents only become irritating when customers cannot understand what you are saying. If your accent is not familiar to the customer, make an extra effort to be clear so that the customer can follow what you are saying.

Painting word pictures

Sell the *sizzle* not the sausage!
Sell the *warmth* not the blanket!
Sell the *sparkle* not the diamond!
Sell the *security* not the insurance!

What do you prefer, someone to describe a film to you or to see it yourself? When you have only words to create a vivid impression in the mind of your customer, your description needs to create a clear impression of what you have to offer. It is important to pay attention to your choice of words and the way in which you say them.

Painting word pictures is the skill that enables you to create positive enticing pictures in the mind of your customer. To communicate successfully on the telephone you need to compensate for the lack of visual stimulus. This means using highly descriptive words that incorporate all the benefits of your product or service. Features describe what a product or service *is*, benefits tell the customer *what's in it for them* if they use a product or service. Customers will not always work out benefits for themselves even if they seem obvious to you. Relate and emphasize the benefits of a product, service or course of action to your customer.

Start by listing the features that you wish to communicate to your customer. They might include the following information:

- The size of your company.
- The experience of its employees.
- The number of satisfied customers that you have.
- The type of product/service that you can offer.
- The range of products or services that you have.
- The geographical distance that you cover.
- The type of after-sales service that you provide.
- The innovations that your company has introduced to enhance quality for customers.

Now choose 'selling' words to describe them. The list below will give you some ideas. Not all of them are relevant but they are all 'selling' words.

special	innovative	breathtaking
authentic	genuine	real
unique	remarkable	guarantee
traditional	fascinating	spectacular
privileged	painstaking	exclusive
powerful	reliable	classic
perfect	exquisite	magnificent
sumptuous	splendour	rich
specialize	flawless	exceptional
distinctive	expert	luxurious
excellence	pure	crafted
finest	stunning	total

Here are some examples below to get you started:

Description: We have remained market leader for over twenty years.
Word picture: As market leader for over twenty years we have established a solid reputation for innovation and the ability to continue to provide our customers with superior products.

Benefit:	So you see Mr/Mrs ... when you buy from us you can be reassured that the decision is a good one because we have a proven record of reliability.
Description:	All our products are handfinished.
Word picture:	What makes our products so distinctive is that they are hand-crafted which makes all of them unique.
Benefit:	So you see Mr/Mrs ... when you buy from us you will know that you are the only person in the world to own such a lovely piece and that really makes it special.

Try out your word pictures on friends and colleagues. To succeed they must be:

- Believable – if you do not believe it, don't say it.
- Brief – what works on the page may not work verbally; avoid wordiness.
- Positive – if you don't sound confident about what you are saying your customer will not be persuaded.

Look for ideas and inspiration in your company's product literature, company brochures or advertising. Select the most potent images. Link the benefit to the word picture. Give your creative talents free rein.

Conversation control

What you say and how you say it are key factors in your conversation with customers. Knowing how to control your own conversation is an important sales skill.

What is conversation control?

It does *not* mean that you control a customer's conversation. Conversation control is the art of controlling *your* conversation in a way that encourages customers to respond to you in a positive and relevant way. It is important because it will enable you to:

- respond to sales objections with confidence;
- avoid being self-defensive;
- extract information quickly;
- sound convincing;
- find out what your customers really want;
- resolve problems expressed by the customer;

- manage situations where conflict arises;
- be assertive not aggressive;
- persuade your customers;
- get the customer to work with you;
- involve your customer in achieving your objectives.

Now consider specific skills of conversation control:

- Direction.
- Challenge.
- Harmony.
- Pace.
- Problem-solving.

Direction

This means the ability to move the conversation from one topic to another by a bridging mechanism. You *steer* the conversation in the direction that you want it to go without being abrupt.

You can move the conversation away from past problems, for example with the product, people or the company, to the present or future. You can link what has happened in the past to what should happen now or in the future. For example:

'Given what you said earlier about our product, how does our new model fit in with your current requirements?'

'How do you think we could modify our delivery schedules to fit in with the orders that are due next month?'

'I am glad that you have highlighted these difficulties, Mr D'Ambrosio, because it gives me the opportunity to tell you about how we can resolve them.'

You can bridge the change of direction by:

- relating what has already happened to the future;
- linking problems to the solutions;
- relating the needs of your customers to your statements;
- moving from a negative stance to a positive one.

Challenge

There may be times when you have to say something that you know will not be well received, for example telling customers that they are going to receive a product later than their requested delivery time. You may have to stand up for your company, challenge the opinions of the customers or question their assumptions.

Customer: 'I feel that compensation is due.'

You: 'Please tell me why you feel that compensation is due?'

A lot of conversations with customers go wrong because salespeople make the wrong assumptions. You may jump to the wrong conclusion if you do not question the customer further to gain more information. Do not accept a customer's opinion without asking for facts or evidence to support that opinion.

Customer: 'That's very expensive.'
You: 'Tell me why you think that it is expensive, Mr D'Ambrosio?'

Stand up for what you want but do not let the conversation descend into a lose-lose situation. Your aim should be to solve the customer's problem and get the best outcome possible for you, the customer and the company. Adopt an assertive, not an aggressive, manner.
   You can state your position in an assertive manner by:

- *summarizing* the situation;
- communicating your *feelings*;
- *stating* your requirements.

You might say something like:

'When you say that our products are inferior [*summary*] it surprises me [*feeling*], that is why I would like to tell you about the quality checks that we have [*statement*]'

Don't offer personal comments like 'You are saying that deliberately to upset me.' This will encourage a negative response from customers who may think that their comments are reasonable and justified. They will also react to your attempts to lay blame on them. No one likes to be put in the wrong.
   Be assertive when:

- you are treated without respect;
- the customer is being contradictory and you want to move the conversation forward;
- the customer makes unsupported, negative comments about your products or services.

Harmony

Customers will not always agree with you. Even when you think that you have identified a way forward they may still have reservations. It is important to remember that they are not directing their criticism at you *personally*. Customers might have a genuine point or they may wish to suggest something that is an improvement on your solution. Nevertheless you must remain in control of your conversation. Reacting to the customer in an over-emotional way only exacerbates the situation and leads to a lose-lose conversation.

You: 'Don't blame me I only work here.'
Customer: 'Who else can I blame when no one takes responsibility in your company?'

Use this three-step approach to maintain harmony with your customer.

1   *Acknowledge* the customer's point of view.
2   *Understand* the customer's position.
3   *Answer* the points the customer has made.

Everyone likes acknowledgement, understanding and answers.

When you *acknowledge* what the customer has said this does not mean that you agree with them. You are acknowledging that you have heard their point and that you are going to take it into account.

'I realize that you feel that this will inconvenience you . . .'

All customers like to be *understood*. It demonstrates your respect for them and helps to build up a good relationship with the customer. It also means that you have listened carefully even if your views differ from the customer.

'I appreciate your concern and I understand the situation you have described is not acceptable to you.'

Now that you have let the customer know that you understand the statement or request you can offer your response. Your answer will be framed to put forward your own perception of the situation and any information that will persuade your customer that the situation is retrievable.

'I think that I can answer that point Mr . . .'

Pace

Conversations can spin out of control when the speed of the conversation increases. This is because you do not have sufficient time to consider your responses. Conversations go too fast when you find yourself offering solutions before you have identified the real problem.

How to slow down the pace

To slow down a conversation, for example when a customer is pressing you for a decision and you feel that you need more information about the situation, you can retrieve control by:

- reflecting back what the customer has said: 'I understand that you want me to replace the product, but to do this I will need more information';
- summarizing the conversation so far: 'Let me recap on the main points that you have made';
- asking the customer a question that will focus the customer's attention on the problem rather than the solution: 'Why do you think that this happened?'

How to increase the pace of the conversation

There will be times when you need to speed up conversations, for example when a customer keeps going over the same ground. Usually when a conversation is going slowly the energy level and interest of you or your customer is low. Your willingness to contribute to the discussion will have an effect on the conversation and boredom or indifference will slow the conversation down. Customers who get stuck in a groove and repeat themselves may need a nudge from you to get things moving again. Choose from one of these methods:

- Say that you want to move on to another item.
- Summarize the conversation and then link to the future: 'What do you want to happen now?'
- Ask your customer how he or she thinks a situation will affect them *personally*. Everyone likes to talk about themselves!
- Ask your customer specific questions.
- Ask your customer for ideas and contribute your own, that is brainstorming.

Problem-solving

In any telephone contact with customers conversations will arise that focus on problems that the customer may be experiencing with your company's employees or its product or services. You may fail to resolve problems if you try to offer a solution before you have fully understood the customer's problem. Jumping in when you think that you have identified a problem can lead to backtracking and going over old ground. You may also suffer a loss of credibility when you get it wrong. You can minimize the risk of the conversation losing its sense of purpose and direction by aiming for a logical flow.

To find out more about the problem you:

- ask questions – summarize;
- identify the problem – summarize;
- summarize what has been said to check understanding.

You can then move the conversation forward to offering a solution. To do this you:

- make suggestions;
- tell the customer what can be done;
- summarize what has been said to check that the customer is satisfied with your proposal.

You can summarize by saying: 'Does that resolve the problem Mr/Mrs...?'

If the customer is still unhappy you have more work to do. Return to identifying the real problem. Offer a solution only when you have identified the real concerns of the customer. If you close the call without checking that you have offered a solution that satisfies the customer, and the problem remains unresolved, your customer may go elsewhere for a satisfactory solution.

Conversation tips and hints

Starting a conversation with a customer is easy when you have a few simple strategies to help you. What you say at the start of the conversation does not have to be clever or full of meaning although it is best not to start on a negative note such as 'I hope that I'm not bothering you.' Think up opening statements around the following:

- The reason you are calling.
- The customer's current situation.
- What you have to offer.

You can start the conversation with:

- a question;
- a fact;
- an opinion.

Your main objective at the beginning of the conversation is to gain the interest and involvement of the customer:

- Talk about a situation you are both involved in.
- Avoid asking customers direct questions about themselves as it may make them feel anxious. Ask questions that will reveal the customer's feelings or opinions on a subject.
- Talking too much about yourself or your company is less likely to involve the customer.

At the start of the conversation your aim is to get customers to tell you what is on their minds. Your opening statement should be short so as to give the customer the opportunity of responding to you immediately. If your opening is too long customers will lose interest and they may feel that you think they have no contribution to make. The sooner the customer is engaged in a conversation with you the more likely it is that the conversation will continue at a relaxed pace. Conversations must be a two-way communication.

Understanding metalanguage

Metalanguage is the term used to define the language chosen by people to convey their meaning which is hidden in the words that are actually spoken. It describes the 'way' something is spoken as well as the actual word content of the conversation. You rely on instinct and sixth sense to understand what the speaker really means. Their language reveals thoughts other than the words actually used.

As an example think of a situation where a shop assistant says 'Can I help you?' and the customer translates the meaning as 'I'd prefer to talk to my friend but I suppose I must serve you.' A good example of how we interpret meaning is how we translate the content of tour operators' brochures, which are worded to make holidays sound more attractive.

Metalanguage	Translation
Sea views	From the attic, if you lean out
Lively resort	Don't bother if you are over eighteen
Plenty of nightlife	The discos are outside your hotel room

Two minutes from the sea	As the crow flies
Unspoilt beaches	Where holidaymakers are packed like sardines
Compact studio apartment	Come alone
En suite facilities	A sink with the plughole missing
Fully furnished	Old and dilapidated furniture
Haute cuisine	Chips with everything

However, if you took all metalanguage from day-to-day conversation you would be left with short and sharp conversation which could sound rude. Metalanguage can soften the real message and allows you or your customers to express emotions without being too blatant.

Emotional involvement in the conversation

The way in which customers refer to an object or person can also reveal their attitudes towards the subject. Words such as 'my', 'the', 'with' and 'to' can reveal underlying feelings about what is said, as in the example below:

Metalanguage	Translation
My company	I'm proud of my company
The company	Which I despise
My car	My pride and joy
The car	It's a company car
I want to talk with you	I'm interested in what you have to say
I want to talk to you	You won't like what I have to say

Emphasis

If you place an emphasis on words when you speak, you can completely change the meaning of a sentence. Check that overemphasis of particular words does not convey a different message to the one that you wish to convey.

Example 1

Words	Message
'I **think** that this is the right course of action for you.'	'I used to be indecisive but now I'm not so sure.'
'I think that **this** is the right course of action for you.'	'and no other'
'I think that this is the **right** course of action for you.'	'If you do otherwise, then you are doing the wrong thing.'
'I think that this is the right course of action for **you**.'	'Any old thing will do for you.'

Example 2

Words	Message
'**I've** always liked you in that dress, the colour really suits you.'	'No one else does.'
'I've always liked **you** in the dress, the colour really suits you.'	'I can't imagine anyone else daft enough to wear it.'
'I've always liked you in that dress, the **colour** really suits you.'	'The style is awful.'
'I've always liked you in that dress, the colour **really** suits you.'	'I'm not being totally honest.'

Clichés

'I mean to say, you know what I mean, sort of – what can I say – you know?'

Using stale and worn out phrases is an easier option than trying to express thoughts clearly and articulately. Clichés can be used to finish a conversation – 'Still, worse things have happened at sea' – or allow someone to offer a cliché of their own – 'Troubles never come by halves, do they?'

Drop clichés, platitudes and tired expressions (okey-dokey?) from your conversation and practise thinking of new ways to express what you want to say. Your customers will respond positively to a conversation that is creative and tailored to them. One conversation does not fit all!

You can irritate customers by using tired worn out phrases such as:

'You know' ('I can't be bothered to express myself clearly')
'Sort of' ('I don't know how to express myself clearly')

Using tired phrases encourages the customer to respond in a similar fashion, for example 'yeah, yeah, I know' so that your conversation has no sense of purpose or direction at all.

Clichés can also give useful clues to the speaker's thoughts. They can be used to play down the importance of what someone is about to say:

'By the way'   'I was just wondering'
'Before I forget'   'Incidentally'
'While I think of it'

These phrases warn you that the words following them are the key words in the statement.

Example 1

'That black outfit you have really suits you: **by the way**, I'm going out on Friday night, could I borrow it?'

Meta-meaning: 'By the way' is used to hide the fact that the request to borrow the outfit is the most important thing being said.

Example 2

'Louise I really appreciate all the overtime you have done for us, (**incidentally**), your request for a holiday has been turned down.'

Meta meaning: 'I've praised your work to sweeten the pill.'

Example 3

'I think we have an agreement, (**oh, while I think of it**) I assume all the delivery charges are included?'

Meta-meaning: 'I know this is unreasonable but if I make it sound a foregone conclusion you might give me what I want.'

Below are some examples of commonly used metalanguage. If you recognize them you are probably using them in your own conversation!

Metalanguage	Meaning
'Honestly', 'absolutely', 'really'	Overemphasis denotes insincerity. 'Frankly I've explored all the options' meaning 'I haven't but it's all you are going to get from me.' Simply saying 'I've explored all the options' is more believable.
'Don't you feel that . . .' 'Don't you think that . . .' 'Isn't it true that . . .'	Listeners are forced to respond with 'yes' even if they disagree with the proposition that is being put to them. 'You want the best for your children, don't you?' is manipulative. Use leading questions with caution. Customers do not like to be manipulated.
'Just', 'only'	Used to minimize the significance of the words that follow: 'I'll only take five minutes of your time' (at least an hour). 'All this for just £10.95' (if you are daft enough to pay it). Can also indicate a lack of confidence: 'I am only new here' (don't blame me if I get it wrong).
'I'll try', 'I'll do my best'	These expressions can predict failure. They can be read as 'I have doubts about my ability to do it.' When the person fails to do what they have been asked they will say 'Well I tried.'
'I'll look into it', 'I'll make every effort'	'If I can pass the buck, I will.'

'Yes, but', 'however', 'still', 'That dress looks very nice but . . .'	'I hate that dress.' Yes, but, however and still lead to the objections that usually follow.
'With respect'	No respect: 'I note your comments but may I say with respect, that I disagree' translates as 'You're talking a load of rubbish'.
'Of course'	Can be used in different ways: 'everyone knows that' (sarcastic); 'I know all there is to know about this subject' (showing off); 'Of course, I expect my usual discount on this order' (introduces an assumption).
'I know that it's none of my business'	I'm going to make it my business anyway.
'Don't get me wrong'	The listener isn't going to like what the speaker has to say but the speaker is going to go ahead and say it anyway.
'Maybe it's not my place to say this'	I'm going to say it anyway.
'Why don't we ask your colleagues?'	Makes the listener's mind search for excuses. 'Let's ask your colleagues' is more likely to get a yes.
'I don't wish to be rude'	I am going to be rude.
'Business is business'	I'm unethical.
'I'll tell you what, I'll think it over and try to get back to you soon'	No thanks – don't call me, I'll call you.
'Let me put it this way'	Here's my version of the truth.

Now practise your metalanguage skills and interpret what is really being said in the statements in Figure 3. Some examples are given to start you off.

When you know what to listen for, understanding metalanguage is not only a useful skill, it can be a lot of fun. Metalanguage is important in maintaining friendly relationships with customers. Listen to the phrases and clichés that you use and eliminate the ones that spoil effective communication. Listen between the lines of what your customers say and you will develop the knack of accurately interpreting the meaning of the message.

Piggybacking

When your conversation becomes stilted and one-sided you can maintain the momentum of a conversation by using the technique of piggybacking:

1 Ask a question.
2 Acknowledge the answer.
3 Ask another question based on your customer's response.

Metastatement	Translation
'I will give the points you have made my urgent attention.'	They are in my pending tray.
'I've nothing against your idea.'	I hate your idea.
'Please don't mind me.'	
'We're all in this together.'	
'That sounds interesting.'	
'They are as good as they were 10 years ago.'	
'It's not that I don't believe you.'	
'I hope that I'm not interrupting . . .'	
'Our sales are up 200 per cent this year.'	
'The meeting was really good and there was a full and frank discussion.'	
'You can be assured of our best service at all times.'	
'We are totally committed to quality.'	
'I'll try to do it as fast as I possibly can.'	
'How interesting you make it sound, tell me more.'	
'I am here to help you.'	

Figure 3   Metalanguage

For example:

Salesperson: 'What type of business are you in Mr James?
Customer: 'We manufacture stationery for personal and commercial use.'
Salesperson: 'I see . . . and how many commercial customers do you have compared to buyers of your personal stationery?'

When you use this technique customers will know from your questions whether you are really listening to their answers. This will encourage them to answer further questions and enable you to develop the conversation.

Conversations often fail because you are so busy trying to think of what you will say next that the customer's response to your initial question goes unheard. This reinforces the customer's perception of you as a poor listener. At the very least you will miss out on valuable clues that will help you to control the direction you want to pursue. Focusing too much on what you want to say will also lead you into repeating yourself and asking the same questions twice – a clear signal to customers that you are not really interested in what they are saying. If customers feel that you are not interested then they will begin to question the relevance of your questions. Linking your questions to the customer's response will help you to avoid interrogating the customer.

Example 1

Salesperson:	'How many did you order last time?'
Customer:	'500 – we already had plenty of stock.'
Salesperson:	'What price did you pay?'
Customer:	'We pay list less 25 per cent.'
Salesperson:	'We couldn't justify that.'
Customer:	'Then there is no point in continuing the conversation, we couldn't justify paying more.'
Salesperson:	'When will you be placing your next order?'
Customer:	'In two weeks, we have a huge new contract that we have just won.'
Salesperson:	'How many will you be ordering?'
Customer:	'Oh, the usual, but like I say, if you can't meet our price there is no point going any further with this.'
Salesperson:	'I understand, but if your regular supplier lets you down you know where we are?'
Customer:	'Yes, thanks for calling.'
Salesperson:	'I'll keep in touch then.'
Customer:	'Yes, do that, bye-bye.'

Now look at how piggybacking helps you to develop the customer's interest in what you have to offer:

Salesperson:	'How many did you order last time?'
Customer:	'500 – we already had plenty of stock.'
Salesperson:	'So you would usually order more?'
Customer:	'Why yes, our usual order is 2000 but things have been quiet lately so we had plenty of stock.'
Salesperson:	'You say things have been quiet lately, what changes are you expecting in the next few months?'
Customer:	'We have just won a huge order so we will be very busy from next month.'
Salesperson:	'That's wonderful, I expect you are very pleased to have won the contract. Given your current stock levels, what will you be ordering next time?'
Customer:	'3000 in the next two weeks.'
Salesperson:	'3000 – will your current supplier have that many in stock?'

Customer: 'We may have a problem there.'
Salesperson: 'You will want to avoid problems occurring for your new customer?'
Customer: 'Yes, it's important we get off to a good start.'
Salesperson: 'Let me explain how I think I can help you get off to a good start. We can...'

The salesperson focuses the conversation on service rather than price. Now that the customer is listening to what she has to say the salesperson has the opportunity to sell the benefits of doing business with her company. The salesperson is selling value, not price.

To develop the conversation further explore your customer's C.O.N.C.E.R.N.S:

- What your customer has currently.
- How the company is organized.
- What needs it has.
- What changes your customer would like to implement.
- What your customer enjoys about the existing arrangements.
- What your customer's reaction is to your offer.
- What new situations your customer has encountered.
- What solution is appropriate.

Silence is golden

Of course, conversational skills are not only confined to what you say, sometimes it's what you don't say that matters! Silence is very effective on the telephone. If a customer is thinking, you *don't* have to fill the void. If a customer makes a request and you don't want to commit yourself, silence can be used to give you time to consider your own opinions or response. Silence can give you time to reflect on what has been said, make a decision or change the subject. Silence is an adaptable conversational tool.

If your customer is silent it may mean that he disagrees with you or that he agrees completely. Try to interpret the meaning of his silence. Silence can have many meanings:

- The customer is thinking about what you have said and is considering your comments.
- The customer is thinking about what you have said and disagrees with your comments.
- The customer is in complete agreement and thinks that there is no need to reply.
- The customer agrees and intends to act on your suggestion.
- The customer agrees but has no intention of acting.
- The customer is too angry to speak.

- The customer hasn't listened and doesn't realize that a response is called for.
- The customer is confused.
- The customer doesn't know how to respond.

If you have made a suggestion *give the customer time to think*. If you rush in with other suggestions you may spoil the moment.

Top tips for conversation winners

1 Be interested not just interesting.
2 Don't jump to conclusions.
3 Avoid dogmatic phrases.
4 Accept ownership of your response.
5 Use 'and' not 'but'.
6 Don't over-react.
7 Defend without being defensive.
8 Discover the problem before you discuss a solution; focus on the future not the past.
9 Co-operate with your customers, don't compete with them.
10 Don't interrupt.
11 Let customers know that you have heard and understood them.
12 Avoid slang, jargon and clichés.
13 Be specific.
14 Speak clearly.

Asking convergent questions

> The art of persuasion is asking the right questions.
>
> (Anon.)

Convergent questions are those that are specific, focused and help you and your customer to come to an agreement. They give your conversation a sense of purpose and direction. Questions can be planned in advance. Although your conversation may take a different course to the one that you had planned, because every customer is different and you cannot predict a customer's answers, 'busking' on the telephone is unwise. If you have worked out some questions in advance you will be more likely to achieve your call objectives.

Convergent questioning is essential to enable you to:

- find out more about what your customer wants or needs;
- clarify any reservations that your customer may have about a proposal;
- gain agreement to your suggestions.

It is a conversational skill not an interrogative tool. Customers generally do not like to be asked a lot of questions especially at a fast pace. Questions should be asked in smooth, low, relaxed voice. Avoid rapid fire questions, allow time for the customer to answer, ask your questions in a conversational manner. When you ask a question *listen carefully* to the answer, it will provide you with clues as to how to proceed. You can avoid sounding like an interrogator by acknowledging an answer to your question before you move on to another question.

As you progress through a call you will want to assess how your customer is reacting. Feedback from your customer will enable you to check your assumptions and help you to minimize misunderstandings. Try some of the questions below to help you to do this.

'Could you explain what you mean by that?'
'You say these problems started when you changed from your usual product?'
'Weren't you about to tell me what happened when . . .'
'Let me summarize what I've understood so far, you say that ... and then ... Is there anything else that you would like to add?'
'Would you clarify that for me?'
'So what you are saying Mrs ... is that you would like ... Is that correct?'
'I'm wondering what it is about my suggestion that you find unacceptable?'
'What are your thoughts about my suggestion?'
'Something seems to be still bothering you, will you tell me what it is?'
'You think my suggestion is basically sound yet you seem to have reservations. What can I do to rectify this?'
'How do you think this will help us to make progress?'
'We've discussed several options, which one do you think will provide the best solution?'
'What specifically has happened to make you feel this way?'

If you ask appropriate and relevant questions you will encourage your customers to be less defensive and they will feel more comfortable about answering. Such questions also enable you to solve problems, keep your conversation impartial and decrease the possibility of your conversation becoming confused.

Open and closed questions

Questions can be broadly categorized as 'open' or 'closed':

- Open questions are designed to extract the maximum amount of information and are mostly used at the start of the call to allow the customer to make a substantial contribution to the conversation.

● Closed questions are useful for confirming information that you have received or to shorten the responses of customers who may be particularly garrulous!

Whilst the concept of open and closed questions is easy to understand, it does require considerable practice to acquire this skill. A useful technique is to practise in role play, the participant who is playing the role of the customer being briefed to respond with 'closed' answers when asked closed questions. For example:

Salesperson: 'Do you use business travel booking facilities?' [closed]
Customer: 'Yes.' [closed answer]

The person playing the role of the salesperson will quickly realize that it is much harder to gather information from a customer if questions are phrased in a closed manner.

Now consider this example where the salesperson asks an open question and the customer responds with an open answer.

Salesperson: 'What sort of business travel booking facilities do you currently use?'
Customer: 'We use booking facilities for flights and accommodation both here and in Europe and the Far East.'

A closed question is easily turned into an open question by adding one or two important words: what, when, where, who and why.

Closed	Open
'Do you use word-processing software?'	'To what extent do you use word-processing software?'
'Do you have any problems with that machine?'	'What has been your experience with that machine?'
'Do you like to travel?'	'How do you feel about travelling?'
'Can the process be improved?'	'How can the process be improved?'
'Did you do that?'	'What did you do?'
'Could you change?'	'What change would work?'
'Are there any other reasons?'	'What other reasons do you have?'

Although asking open questions does not guarantee that your customer's responses will be open (customers may still respond with the minimum of information if they are naturally unforthcoming!) it will increase the possibility of you gaining the information that you require. Once you have mastered the basic technique of open and closed questions you can progress to more complex questions.

Alternative questions

These questions encourage customers to make decisions. You offer a choice and customers select the option that interests them most. This is a form of closed question but it has the advantage that it can significantly progress your call.

Salesperson: 'Which would you prefer, Mr Smith, the pink one or the blue one?'
Customer: 'The blue one.'

Leading questions

The context, wording and inflection of a leading question can cause customers to think that there is only one answer and that is 'yes'. However, be selective in your use of such questions as they can be interpreted by the customer as manipulative.

Salesperson: 'You want good quality at an affordable price, don't you?'
Customer: 'Yes.'

Hypothetical questions

Hypothetical questions can be closed or open and are terrific for opening up conversation and breaking deadlocks. You can divert customers from a negative frame of mind to a positive one by suggesting hypothetical situations for them to consider. This type of question also has the advantage that you can select a scenario that gives you the opportunity to illustrate the superiority of your product or service in the areas where it is most competitive. Use 'What if' and 'Let's suppose that' to introduce your hypothesis.

Salesperson: 'I appreciate that you are happy with your present supplier, Mrs Latham, however, you did mention how important guaranteed delivery dates were to you so that you could meet your commitments to your own customers. Let's suppose that for some reason your supplier could not guarantee a delivery date, what alternative sources would you consider?'
Customer: 'I guess I would have to try to find another supplier but they would have to be reliable, we can't afford to be let down.'
Salesperson: 'That is where I think we could help you, Mrs Latham, we can . . .'

Prompting questions

These questions are phrased so that the customer is encouraged to volunteer 'free' information. Prompt uncommunicative customers to be more forthcoming. Some customers need help to continue with their story, or they may respond in a literal way to your questions confining what they say to providing specific information. In a sales call you can use prompts to oil the wheels of a conversation.

Salesperson:	'That's very interesting, Mr Jackson, so tell me what happened then?'
Customer:	'Well . . .'

Other useful phrases are 'Tell me more about that' and 'Describe that to me'.

Look at the questions below and consider which of the question types discussed above these questions fall into.

Question   **Type**

'Would you like it delivered today or tomorrow?'

'So you really would make savings on your time, wouldn't you?'

'Do you normally place your orders with one supplier?'

'How do you usually deal with this situation?'

'If you were looking for another supplier, what would you be looking for?'

'How would you like to pay, cash or account?'

'What happened then?'

'I think this is what you want, isn't it?'

'Did you return the faulty goods to us?'

'What did you do first when it broke down?'

'If you had the budget available would you do this?'

Although you will move from one type of question to another during the course of the conversation and pre-planning is limited in the sense that every call is or should be different (all customers are unique), it is helpful to have a portfolio of useful questions that will enable you to keep the conversation going. There are some suggestions below but, of course, you are free to devise your own. Find the questions that work for you.

Seven useful open questions

Tuck away these seven versatile open questions for future use in almost any situation.

1   'Tell me more about your company Mr/Mrs ... what do you specialize in?'
2   'What can we do to improve the level of service that you currently have?'
3   'What changes do you anticipate in the next six months?'
4   'How do you feel about changing your present arrangements?'
5   'What is your point of view on your current situation?'
6   'What improvements would you like to see?'
7   'What key factors will influence your decision?'

To improve your questioning skills listen to radio and television interviewers. Identify what questions work for them and learn to recognize the question types that have been discussed here. How is the interviewee's response affected by the question?

How to use active listening to identify business opportunities

Research has shown that people spend 70–80 per cent of their waking hours in verbal communication, nearly half of this time is spent listening.

A number of interpersonal skills are involved in meeting the expectations of your customers and one of the most important of these is using 'active listening' to demonstrate to customers that they are important to you and your company.

What is active listening?

Many people believe that listening occurs when they hear others speaking. However, the reception of sound should not be confused with active listening, which requires *conscious perception* of what the other person is saying. Listening is deliberate, *active* behaviour. It means becoming involved in the conversation, demonstrating interest in what is being said and paying attention to the *context* of the conversation. Active listening requires concentration. You search for meaning and understanding, and this energy and effort is potentially tiring because it is hard work to listen well. The high level of concentration that is required is one of the reasons why those engaged in outbound calling feel so exhausted at the end of the day. Active listening enables you to:

- help your customers to 'tell their story';
- focus your full attention on what the customer is saying;
- interpret correctly the context and meaning of what the customer is saying;
- organize information so that you can make sense of complex or badly structured conversations;
- minimize personal bias and avoid stereotyping customers.

Look at the list below and consider your current listening skills. The list may give you some ideas about which listening habits you are happy with and those you might wish to change.

1   Do you assume that you know what the customer is going to say?
2   Do you listen to the customer's point of view even if it is different from your own?
3   Do you restate instructions and responses to be sure that you have understood them correctly?
4   Do you try to learn something new from each customer that you talk to?
5   Do you check your understanding when customers use words that are unfamiliar to you?
6   Do you get defensive while the customer is still talking?
7   Do you always concentrate on what is being said even if you've heard it all before?
8   Do you daydream when a customer is talking?
9   Do you listen only to what you want to hear?
10   Do you interrupt customers when they are speaking?
11   Do you take notes when necessary to help you to remember the important details of a conversation.
12   Do you allow background noise in the office to distract you?
13   Do you listen to a customer without judging or criticizing them?
14   Do you tune out when customers say something you don't want to hear?

You can improve your listening skills by:

- being patient and avoiding the temptation to interrupt;
- summarizing as you progress through your conversation;
- thinking before you speak;
- prompting customers to tell their stories and allowing them time to finish;
- empathizing with the customer;
- concentrating on the call and avoiding distractions in the office;
- showing interest in the outcome of the call;
- giving full attention to what is being said rather than thinking about how you are going to respond;

- asking customers about their feelings;
- being non-judgmental;
- keeping an open mind;
- allowing the customer to do the talking.

There are four main types of active listening:

1 You listen for *pleasure*, for example to poetry or music.
2 You listen to *comprehend* what is being said, you try to understand facts, ideas and themes.
3 You listen with *empathy*, demonstrating your willingness to understand the thoughts and feelings of your customer.
4 You listen to *assess* what is being said to determine the strengths and weaknesses of an argument; you listen for the main points of an argument.

Your motivation will affect how well you listen. If you are feeling tired you will find it more difficult to concentrate. Background noise and lack of ventilation can interfere with active listening. If you are in an open plan office encourage your colleagues not to disturb you while you are making calls. If you do not listen actively you will miss sales opportunities or problems that the customer is discussing with you. You can aid concentration by asking yourself questions such as 'Why is the customer telling me this?' Create mental pictures of what the customer is saying. Taking notes can also help you concentrate. If you do take notes beware of concentrating so hard that the customer starts to wonder if you are listening. It is advisable to tell the customer that you are taking notes and that if there is a silence it is because you are listening attentively.

Useful listening techniques

1 Preparation

Prioritize complex calls for a time when you are least likely to be stressed or tired. Make a conscious effort to put aside preoccupations such as forthcoming holidays or personal concerns. Try to arrange your environment so that you are not likely to be distracted and will be able to concentrate on what your customer is saying.

2 Following

One of the prime objectives of listening is to discover your customers' views on what is being discussed. If you interrupt customers by asking too many questions or making too many remarks you may confuse the issues. Encourage customers to talk by using verbal prompts such as 'mmm', 'really', 'yes', 'and . . .', 'tell me more', 'I see'. These signal to customers that you are listening and this will encourage them to continue. If you remain silent for too long the speaker may feel the need to ask 'Are you still there?' Verbal prompts let customers know that you have heard them and that you want to hear more. You can also try accenting a word that customers have used to encourage them to elaborate on what they have said.

Customer:	'Your proposal seems OK.'
You:	'*Seems* OK?'
Customer:	'Well, I suppose so, it's just that I wondered if it would be possible to . . .'

You can reflect back statements that customers have made to demonstrate that you have understood and are following their points. Reflection also provides customers with the chance to clarify their own thoughts. Use 'You feel . . . because . . .' as an easy and useful way of confirming feelings and facts.

Listen for clues

Clues are the words used by customers to draw attention to what they feel is important. They do this not only with their choice of words but also with the tone of voice that they use. You are given clues each time you have a conversation with a customer. If you are under pressure you will not give customers your full attention and may miss opportunities to identify solutions. Customers do not always spell things out. You need to show an interest and invite them to say more on the matter.

The use of the words 'I', 'me' or 'my' is indicative of a strongly held view and reveals the extent of customers' personal involvement in the subject under discussion. Customers may use words like 'angry', 'upset', 'happy', 'excited' or 'enthusiastic'. Such words describe their emotions about the issue being discussed, they are 'key' words. You can find out more by asking customers what they mean by their use of the key word, for example 'What has made you so upset?' Customers can indicate being under pressure themselves, 'I can't let this happen, my manager will be furious.' Listen carefully to the customer's tone of voice and what words are emphasized. Voice tone will indicate whether a customer is indifferent to or passionate about a subject.

Listening is an undervalued skill, one that is easily taken for granted. Active listening is not the same as hearing what a customer says to you. It requires effort and input from you. Poor listening leads to missed sales opportunities and creates a bad impression with customers. If you don't listen actively this communicates itself to customers as indifference to them.

Top tips for becoming a competent listener

1   Recognize the main points that the customer is making.
2   Recall the basic details of the conversation accurately.
3   Listen with an open mind.
4   Distinguish between fact and opinion.
5   Differentiate between emotional and logical arguments.
6   Recognize bias and prejudice.
7   Understand the customer's attitude.
8   Review what has been said impartially.

What is effective sales communication?

First, a definition of sales communication:

> Sales communication is the passing of information from one party to another, with the express aim of persuading customers to take a course of action they might not otherwise take.

The key word to remember is action. Without action there is no sales communication . . . just talking.

Customers do not always know what they want, and if you listen inactively, you will fail to help them properly. Equally, if you fail to get your message across in terms that are easily understood by customers, they will be confused and may misunderstand the key points of the call. This can lead to further problems especially if the misunderstandings relate to terms and conditions of the provision of your products or services. A simple rule of effective sales communication is to keep it simple and don't use several words where one will do.

To ensure that your customers take the correct action, and know what action they are going to get, you need to ask yourself the following questions before completing a telephone call.

Does your customer know:

● What is going to happen?
● How it is going to happen?
● When it is going to happen?
● Where it is going to happen?
● Who is going to make it happen?

If you haven't satisfied these requirements, then your customer will be in doubt. If you have met them and the customer is happy with the planned action, then your next step is to make sure it happens. That's effective sales communication.

Steps for effective sales communication

Don't sit back and hope your sales message has been communicated. Check and make the communication work.

Step 1   Check that you have communicated your message in a way that is clear and unambiguous.

Step 2   Check that the customer has heard you correctly.

Step 3   Check that the customer has understood what you have said.

Step 4   Check that the customer has accepted your proposal.

Step 5   Check that the customer takes the appropriate action to make it happen.

Why sales communication fails

How often have you called on customers . . .

- to find they are not in, when you call;
- to learn that they were expecting you earlier or later;
- to find they were not expecting you that day.

If you can answer 'yes' to any of these you are not communicating effectively. Communications usually fail because you:

- don't ask enough questions;
- listen inactively;
- make assumptions;
- don't use the same language (misunderstanding);
- use slang, lazy phrases, jargon;
- don't check that you and your customer are in agreement on the precise action that is to be taken.

Avoid baffling your customers by using overlong words which can confuse your meaning. Keep your descriptions simple and easy to understand. Use short words rather than long ones:

Additional	More	Despatch	Send
Alteration	Change	Manufacture	Make
Anticipate	Predict	Merchandise	Sell
Assistance	Help	Numerous	Many
Facilitate	Ease	Objective	Fair
Considerable	Ample	Fundamental	Key
Commencement	Start		

Use one or two words rather than several:

According to our records – We know
A large majority of – Most
A percentage of – Some
Along the lines of – Like
At this precise moment in time – Now
Due to the fact that – Because
Facilities are provided for . . . – We can . . .
Generally speaking in this connection – Usually
I am inclined to the view that – I think
In the event that the foregoing – If
In the not too distant future – Soon
Prior to this we experienced – Previously
I am prepared to admit – I'm sorry

Effective sales communication means thinking carefully about the message you wish to convey to your customers. It requires concentration and the willingness to listen carefully for clues as to how your customer feels about a situation or proposal. On the telephone the words that you use have the power to create strong responses in your customers, so make sure that they are positive ones. Analyse how a meaning can be enhanced through the careful choice of words. Look for inspiration in the work of copywriters who make every word count.

5   The essential rules of customer engagement

This chapter is intended to underline the importance of making every contact with customers count. There are two fundamental questions you should always ask:

Why are you calling?
What are you going to say?

Telephone sales calls fail when they are not planned and when insufficient time is spent thinking about how to get the message across. One manager who asked her team these questions got a different reply from every member of the team even though they were working on the same customer base and selling the same products. To achieve consistency and competence calls should be prepared, have objectives and be structured.

Setting objectives

Every call should progress you further towards a sale. Measure your success by identifying what you have achieved with every contact that you make. For example a cold call that results in you learning about the structure of a company and the key players in the decision-making process is clearly a progressive step.

To help you to prepare satisfactorily and identify your objectives, consider your overall sales objectives, the type of call you are making and how you can progress the sale or your relationship with customers from the point they are at now.

To be fully prepared for any questions that the customer may want to put to you check that you:

- have set yourself objectives for the call;
- have up-to-date product knowledge;
- have a clear idea of the features and benefits of your product or service;
- know which of these are unique to your business;
- are fully conversant with any special promotions or offers that are currently available;
- have alternative strategies if your plan fails; and
- have up-to-date pricing.

Whilst you will not know precisely what objections the customer may express, none the less there are some that will become familiar to you through repetition. Keep all relevant material that will help you to counteract resistance readily available and up to date. Quoting testimonials that are 10 years old does not convince customers. Rather they could imagine that no one has had a good word to say about you in the last 10 years. Not the message that you intended to convey.

Call type	Activity
Prospecting	<ul><li>List cleaning</li><li>Updating customer database records</li><li>Mailshot or brochure follow-up calls</li><li>Cold-calling</li><li>Market research</li></ul>
Maintaining contact with existing customers	<ul><li>Welcome calls</li><li>Care calls</li><li>Up-selling and cross-selling</li><li>Renewal business</li></ul>
Key account management	<ul><li>Building customer relationships</li><li>Updating customers on product and service changes that may affect them</li><li>Identifying 'decision-makers' and 'influencers'</li><li>Handling customer complaints and concerns</li><li>Negotiating</li></ul>
Appointment-making	<ul><li>Identifying sales opportunities</li><li>Making qualified appointments</li><li>Following up marketing initiatives, e.g. advertising, mailings, brochures, exhibitions</li></ul>

Figure 4   Call types

Setting objectives for your call will give you a sense of purpose and direction. You can measure your progress on managing your sales activities if you have clearly defined goals. Your overall sales objectives can focus on specific or general goals:

- Specific goals: to increase the volume of orders by 50 per cent; to increase the value of orders by 25 per cent.
- General goals: to sell more products across the range to existing customers; to sell to more people, that is increase the number of customers that you have.

Now consider the type of call that you are making. Figure 4 provides a typical range of call types and the activities involved. (In Chapter 7 instructions will be given on how to create a call plan that will enable you to establish how much time you would spend on each activity.) The objectives of some of these activities and call types are discussed below.

Welcome calls

The primary objective of welcome calls is:

> to ensure that customers' first experience of the company is a positive one and that their expectations are met.

Secondary objectives include the following:

- Identify further opportunities to do business.
- Give the customer a point of contact with the company.
- Familiarize the customer with relevant company procedures.

Care calls

The primary objective of care calls is:

> to update customers on new products, services or procedures and alleviate any problems that they may have experienced.

Secondary objectives include the following:

- To confirm that the information you have about the customer is correct.

- To establish whether changes in the customer's circumstances present other business opportunities.

Major accounts

The primary objective of major account calls is:

to consolidate your relationship with the customer and maintain awareness of competitor activity which has the potential to threaten your position as a supplier.

Secondary objectives include the following:

- To inform the customer of promotional offers.
- To explore opportunities to increase the amount of business.
- To get referrals to other divisions of the company.
- To familiarize yourself with customers' markets and their products and services.
- To establish your company as sole supplier.
- To ensure that all contacts who have an influence on the buying decision have a regular call from you.

Other customers' calls

The primary objective of calls to other customers is:

to identify those customers who have the potential for growth and to maintain their commitment to your company.

Secondary objectives include the following:

- To demonstrate your commitment to customers and show your appreciation of their custom.
- To maximize the level of business that the customers do with you.
- To ensure that you call frequently enough to prevent customers from feeling that you take their business for granted.
- To keep up to date with changes in your customers' businesses or markets.

Prospecting (cold calls)

The primary objective of cold-calling is:

to increase your customer base and avoid attrition of your current sales through lost business.

Secondary objectives include the following:

- To identify your competitors.
- To identify areas where your company has something to offer that is measurably different to what the prospect already has.
- To introduce the prospect to the benefits of doing business with your company.
- To win new business.

List cleaning

The primary objective of list cleaning is:

> to correct any errors of information that you have about the prospect so that all communications both written and verbal are professionally presented.

A secondary objective is:

- To reduce the amount of time wasted talking to the wrong people about the wrong product or service.

You may be thinking that the primary objective of any call is to make a sale and you would be right. However, every call that you make will not result in a sale, although it would be wonderful if they did. A more realistic approach is to measure your progress in terms of achieved objectives so that you can enjoy success as you move nearer to achieving your ultimate goal – a sale.

Developing a structured approach

Every call that you make will benefit from a structured approach. Sales are lost because customers either do not understand the benefits of a proposition or they do not see the relevance of your proposition to their situation and therefore are unwilling to listen to your proposal. Before you make a diagnosis take time to ask questions and get to know more about the customer's priorities and concerns. A structured call will enable you to match your pace to that of the customer and it will help you to choose those benefits that are most likely to overcome indifference. To test the logic of the sequence of your call ask yourself the following questions:

- Will customers answer questions if there is no rapport between them and the salesperson?
- Will customers buy a product or service if they perceive no need for it (or want)?

- Will customers buy if they think the product or service provides no real improvement on their current arrangements?
- Will customers buy if they think that the product or service does not offer value for money?
- Will they buy if the time is not right?
- Will they buy if a salesperson does not ask for an order?

Your answers will already be suggesting the sequence of a sale to you:

1   Establish a rapport.
2   Gather more information about your customer.
3   Establish a need (or a want).
4   Tell customers what's in it for them – sell the benefits of your proposition.
5   Emphasize value rather than cost.
6   Persuade customers that the time to buy is now.
7   Ask for the order. Gain commitment.

This sequence may not take place in one telephone call, indeed it is highly unlikely that it will. It is important to know at which point in the sequence you are during the sales process otherwise you may race ahead trying to close when the customer still has not perceived a need for your product or service. A notable exception is the publishing market where unsold advertising space represents lost revenue that can never be recovered once the publication hits the stands. Telephone salespeople will try very hard to close on the first call to a prospective advertiser. Perhaps this is why this sector has gained a reputation for 'hard selling'. The following quote is from an experienced newspaper sales executive who now works for a company that sells computer technology. She starts by speaking about her previous job in advertising sales.

> For training we used to go to the Birmingham office It was in-house training and they gave us quite harsh techniques of how to close, how to open, how to get your foot in the door when you were cold-calling. We would make out that the customer's company wasn't suitable to be advertising in the feature and maybe they should wait for another feature. It makes the company think 'Well, excuse me, it's only advertising' and 'I want to take that space because my company is as good as the rest of them.'
>   I've never had the confidence to use that kind of technique anyway because I thought it was a bit condescending to the customer. Basically you're telling them that their company is not good enough to advertise in the newspaper. I think for the first couple of days you think, 'Yes, it would work', but then you tend to think 'No, it doesn't', in reality customers don't like the abruptness and they don't like the directness. I don't think anybody does and I always thought it was easier to cushion what you were selling to them than actually going directly in for the kill. I

would befriend the customer, tell them what we were doing, tell them why I thought this was appropriate for their company and in fact do the reverse of what I was taught to do. I would tell them the benefits, that's the way I did it and it used to work for me. I mean everybody's different, we all closed in different ways. Some of them were direct saying, 'I've got this advertising space, I know you advertised last week, shall I fit the same advert in this space?' Everybody in the newspaper was totally different, we all had our own selling techniques.

The selling that I'm doing now is basically selling to customers who have already purchased systems from us. The customer wants our products, the market is niched for us whereas in advertising you had to hit everybody and anybody. I like the position I'm in now because you're speaking to customers on a regular basis, you can build a rapport up with them and you get to know them and you get to know what they want, whereas cold-calling it's 'wham bam, thank you ma'am' and see you next time when you want to advertise.

(Ex-advertising telephone sales executive)

'SMILE'

The 'SMILE' sequence has been devised to help you to structure your calls in a way that leads the conversation in a purposeful manner and will cover all the aspects of the call that we have already discussed. This mnemonic has been chosen because not only is it memorable but it also recalls one of the oldest pieces of advice given to telephone salespeople – 'Smile when you dial'. It can be easily adapted to accommodate most types of outbound calling whether a sale or an appointment is the desired outcome.

When you SMILE you:

Start with a rapport;
Maximise the contact;
Introduce a solution;
Look for agreement;
End on a positive note.

This structure will enable you to approach the different steps of the sale in a logical sequence, which may not be completed until some time after your first contact. It will give your calls a sense of purpose and direction and help you to avoid unstructured rambling calls that go nowhere and leave the customer confused.

Now let's look at each stage in more detail.

Start with a rapport

Unless a rapport is established with your customer your call is not going to continue. Customers are reluctant to engage in conversation with people who they feel are more interested in their own agenda than the customer's concerns. You can establish a rapport with the customer by asking questions that may not be specifically business related. For example you may start the call with a reference to the customer's recent holiday. However, you must be clear about how far you want the call to go in this direction. If you find yourself discussing the merits of one particular beach compared to another you are having a chat and not selling. Be interested but professional; if you get too intimate with a customer you could lose credibility and when the call becomes complex the customer may want to speak to a 'manager' or 'someone in authority'. Pleasantries oil the wheels of the conversation, but they must be balanced with achieving sales objectives. There is nothing more frustrating than a customer saying 'Well, it's been lovely chatting to you but I really must go now.' It is too late to get the conversation back on track and you might even reply: 'Oh, right, but I really wanted to talk to you about...' This response puts you on a deadline that makes it impossible to do your call justice.

The 'verbal handshake'

This is a useful technique to establish rapport. Just as we take time to 'settle' into a conversation when we meet customers face-to-face we must start our telephone conversation in an unhurried but purposeful manner. You wouldn't barge straight into a room and start firing questions at customers without introducing yourself first – so why do it on the telephone? Most introductions to customers are conducted at the speed of light. Remember to slow down a little, use a calm confident tone of voice. *Expect* the customer to give you their full attention. Introduce yourself (give your full name, for example Mary Johnson) and say why you are calling and where you are calling from.

Check that the customer is free to speak to you if you aren't sure. If customers are pressed for time they will appreciate your courtesy and are unlikely to refuse to speak to you again. Make a telephone appointment to call again and get off the line. No one is going to pay attention to what you have to say if they have one eye on the clock. Speak to customers who have the time to speak to you. If you press on regardless you run the risk of annoying customers and will find it difficult to be put through to them in the future.

Relax, if you have something important to say the customer will listen. Your call should be approached from the point of view that what you have to say will benefit the customer. The call is a service to the customer in that it will allow the customer to consider another option for a product or service that their company requires.

If it is appropriate, refer to the last conversation that you had with the customer or if it is the first time that you have spoken, ask about something that will interest the customer to get the conversation started. Use the customer's name. This personalizes the call and establishes a rapport with the customer from the outset. However, don't use it too much, be natural. Otherwise you will turn customers off with your insincerity. It is also worth remembering that some customers do not respond well to the indiscriminate use of their first name. Take your cue from the customers, if they use your first name then it is acceptable for you to respond in a similar fashion. Avoid using the designation sir or madam as this sounds too impersonal, as if you can't be bothered to address them on a more personal basis.

You never get a second chance to make a first impression. From the moment you start talking to your customers you should be consciously setting out to make a good impression. How you sound will also influence customers' responses – if you are lukewarm they will be cold. *Enthusiasm is infectious.*

Evolve an interesting and compelling approach at the outset to encourage customers to focus on what you are saying. This approach could be based on one of the following:

- A fact that you have discovered about their business.
- A referral from someone they know in another company.
- A follow-up call to a letter you have written to the customer recently.
- A new product or service that you are offering.
- Something topical you have read about (change in legislation, etc.).
- Changes that have taken place in your business since you last spoke.

Keep your introduction brief and simple, you want to encourage your customer to talk. If you do all the talking they will give up listening! Try to engage the customer in the conversation right at the outset. Some customers may have a low threshold of attention. You can help to maintain it if you allow them to contribute to the call. Let customers know that they have your undivided attention. Focus on the customers, sound interested in their responses.

Now you are ready to progress to the next step.

Maximize the contact

Maximizing the contact means making the most of your conversations with customers so that every call progresses you along the sales continuum. It would be nice if every call you made resulted in a sale but this is not realistic, even if sales managers would like you to think it is! Calls that do not attempt to maximize the contact are a waste of your time and the customer's. Just as a doctor needs to diagnose an illness before offering a cure, you will need to spend some time talking to customers about their current arrangements before you can identify needs or problems that can be resolved by your product or service.

This stage of the call will also help you to identify opportunities to do more business by exploring areas where the customer may have the need for other products or services in your range. If you develop an easy-going conversational style you will avoid sounding like a grand inquisitor. Don't put your customer in the dock. If you fire questions at customers without acknowledging their responses, they will quickly become uncomfortable and may want to end the call, especially if they do not understand why you are asking certain questions. It always helps to put your questions into context. In other words, explain the reason for your questions and what you expect to be able to do with the information.

In the early stages of the call ask open-ended questions which encourage customers to talk about themselves and enable you to gather the maximum amount of information. If you think you have spotted a need, don't jump in too quickly – take your time. In this stage of your conversation the emphasis is on asking questions and gathering information that will help you to identify where your product or service is going to be most beneficial to the customer. Ask enough questions to give the whole picture. This will help you to select the solution that best matches the customer's needs.

Ways to maximize the contact

- Identify all those in the company who are potential customers of your business.
- Establish what the customer does now.
- Find out more about the problems that customers may have experienced with their current arrangements.
- Look for the opportunity to put forward a proposal or a quotation.
- Discuss your customers' opinions about your own products and services.
- Find out when the customer is buying.
- Create a positive impression of your company even if the opportunity to do business is minimal.
- If your call is to an existing customer check that the customer is happy with what you have done to date and ask what the customer would like in the future.

Now that you have gathered sufficient information to enable you to put forward a positive case for the customer to consider purchasing from you, it is time to progress to the next step.

Introduce a solution

If you have gathered the right information you will now be in a position to present your product, service or proposal and to relate its benefits to your customer.

When you introduce a solution, adopt a 'partnership' approach to your customer's needs. Don't offer the solution that suits you best if it conflicts with your customer's interests. Involve the customer in this process so that you work as partners together.

Link phrases to lead you into introducing a solution that is the best 'match' for the customer.

'Well Mr/Mrs ... from what you have told me it sounds as if our ... would suit you.'

Don't tell customers everything you know, use only the information that is relevant to them. Avoid the temptation to rush this stage, remember that if you have got this far your customer is clearly interested in what you have to say.

Summarize your proposal and finish with a benefit, show customers *what is in it for them*.

'So Mr/Mrs ... I hope that you can see that buying our software will increase the productivity of your computers without resorting to expensive up-grading, which means that you will increase efficiency without unnecessary capital expenditure.'

The solution that you select must be appropriate to the circumstances of the customer. If you succumb to the temptation to 'oversell' you may not be able to return to that customer. It's important to build a long-term relationship with your customers even if it may be a long time before they repurchase. A positive impression of you and your company will influence how they describe you to other potential customers, and often as much business comes from referrals as it does from advertising and other marketing activities.

Can you immediately respond to the question 'Why should I buy from you?' If you hesitated, consider this – if you can't think of a single reason why customers should buy from you, then why on earth should they? You are your company's advocate and as such you are responsible for presenting the strengths of your company. Let your competitors worry about weaknesses. No company sets out to fail, most want to develop into profitable organizations with long-term prospects. Your company will have assessed the market in which you operate and will have attempted to provide goods and services at a competitive price, plus features that it hopes will separate it from its competitors. You need to understand how you stack up against the options available to your customers.

Typical solutions could centre around the following:

Extra features	Unique product or service
Improved credit terms	Experience of customer's market or business
More comprehensive service package	Stock availability
Better pricing	After-sales service
Wider range of goods or services	Customer care
Technical superiority	Minimum order quantities

Select only the solution that is appropriate to the customer. Make sure that you have a 'feel' for what will appeal to the customer. For example customers who are timid will not find the idea of dealing with an innovative organization particularly attractive. They would probably prefer a tried and tested solution which carries fewer risks at the expense of being the first in the market to use the solution. Therefore it would be sensible to focus on the customers who have successfully used the product so that the timid customer is reassured that choosing you is in fact a 'safe' option.

To introduce successful solutions link *specific* benefits of your product or service to your customer and mention the *unique points* about your product or service that differentiates you from the competition.

- Sell on the strengths of your solution, not the weaknesses of your competition.
- Be confident, but don't be tempted to exaggerate.
- Use the experience of other customers and your own research to support your proposition.

Sometimes a solution is not readily suggested to you. If this is the case then you can use your customers' ideas to help you. Ask your customers what improvements to their current arrangements they would like. Listen carefully and try to identify where your products or service can help.

Even if you cannot readily identify something that differentiates your company from its competition, there is one unique difference – you. Customers like to do business with people that they like and trust. Their relationship with suppliers is important. Tell your customer about what you can do as an individual to help them in their business.

Remember to *paint the picture – tell the story*. This is the pure selling stage of the call. It is here that you will use your word power and persuasiveness to create an attractive desirable picture of what your company has to offer.

Now that you have found something to offer your customer it is time to test whether your proposal or solution is acceptable to the customer.

Look for agreement

Even if you are sure that the solution that you have selected is the best one for your customer, you must check that your customer agrees with you! Do this by testing the customer's response with 'trial' closes . For example:

'Do you agree with that?'
'Am I right in assuming that this is what you are looking for?'
'Do you think that will solve the problem?'

If the customer agrees with you on each point as it is discussed it will make the final decision easier for the customer to make. Trial closing is effective at gaining commitment in small steps as you progress though the conversation. If you do have a disagreement you can answer each point as it occurs rather than risk being faced with a barrage of objections at the end of your conversation.

You can refer to the points that you agreed as an introduction to your closing statement.

'Well Mr/Mrs ... you said earlier that you need to enhance the performance of your computers, our software would help you to do that wouldn't you agree?'

or

'You told me earlier that you would like to order in smaller batches so our minimum order quantity of 10 would suit you very well. Do you agree?'

You can move to the close of the call when you have achieved the following:

- You have identified what the customer wants or needs.
- You have successfully identified a solution.
- The customer has agreed that he or she is interested.

Use phrases like:

'So, when would you like us to start Mr/Mrs ...'
'I am expecting the new stock tomorrow Mr/Mrs ... would you like me to reserve some for you?'
'Which week would you like us to begin?'
'When would you like it to be delivered, this week or next week?'

Don't be afraid to ask for a decision, the worst that can happen is that the customer says no! One useful tip is to lower your voice at the close. Sound unhurried – confident.

Use the following techniques to help you close successfully.

The compromise close

Give customers the feeling that you want to meet them halfway to secure their orders. Everyone likes a bargain. Try to tie your offer to a fast decision.

'How about this Mr / Mrs . . . if you place an order for 10 items today I will let you have them at 10 per cent discount.'

The choice close

Offer options that require the customer to make a commitment, for example 100 or 200, pink or blue, this week or next week.

'Mr / Mrs . . . we can provide these in pink or blue, which colour would you like?'

The do it now close

Prices go up from time to time so give your customers the chance to buy before they do. Use word pictures to create vivid pictures in the customer's mind of the consequences for his business if he doesn't BUY NOW.

'I'll get this order progressed today Mr / Mrs . . . I know that we have a price increase coming up soon and because you need to budget so tightly at the moment it makes sense to order now, doesn't it?'

The direct close

The simplest close of all. Ask for the order.

'How many do you want?'

The puppy-dog close

Let the customer use your products to trial them before buying. The idea is that the customer will fall in love with them and won't want to give them back. Just like a puppy!

The fear factor close

Every customer wants products or services that reduce risk and increase their chance to prosper. If the customers don't buy from you then something unexpected may happen and they will not be equipped to cope with it.

'If your computer suffered from a virus that you couldn't detect, it would be very expensive down time, wouldn't it? That is why the sooner you have this installed the less exposed you will be to this risk. Is tomorrow convenient for you?'

The assumptive close

Say to yourself that the customer has already bought. This is a good close for indecisive and reluctant customers.

'When I receive your order I will make sure that it is processed immediately.'
'I will put your order on our system and you can expect delivery by the end of the week.'

The action close

You get your customers physically involved in the sales process. Ask them to leaf through your catalogue with you, fax something to you or write out their requirements there and then.

The callback close

Customers may want to confer with someone else before making a decision. You can try to gain commitment from them so that you can order on a 'subject to approval' basis. When you call back start by asking for the order. Don't ask them if they have thought about it, the answer will invariably be no!

'Good morning Mr/Mrs ... we spoke yesterday about an order for two dozen binding machines. When would you like us to deliver them?'

The qualifying close

Make customers feel that they have qualified to be a member of an exclusive club.

'Now that you have exceeded our qualifying minimum order quantity you are entitled to an extra 10 per cent discount. How many would you like to order?'

Once you have got your order you can then

End on a positive note

Use the following guidelines to ensure that you end on a positive note. Reassure customers by your manner and actions that they have made the right decision.

1 Confirm what action is required by your customer and what you will do.
2 Thank customers for their business, for example 'I'm so pleased that you have decided to go ahead Mr/Mrs ... I know that you will be very happy with your new system.'
3 Check that you have the correct contact/delivery details.
4 If you are calling the customer back agree a time and date that is convenient to the customer.

Start with a rapport	yes/no	yes/no	yes/no	yes/no	yes/no
Prepared for call					
Verbal handshake					
Used positive language					
Used customer's name					
Maximize the contact					
Gathered information					
Developed conversation					
Searched for sales opportunities					
Identified needs					
Introduce a solution					
Used features					
Used benefits					
Painted word pictures					
Proposed a solution that matches the needs of the customer					
Look for agreement					
Established that your customer agreed with your proposition					
Gained commitment					
Dealt with customer's concerns					
End on a positive note					
Gave point of contact					
Thanked customer for time					
Agreed future action					

Figure 5   SMILE checklist

Use the 'SMILE' construct to ensure that your contact with customers is positive and that your calls to customers have a sense of direction and purpose. Show your customers that you are 'a good company to do business with'. Even if your calls do not end with an immediate order, leave the customer with a positive impression of you and your company. The customer does ultimately have the right to say no. Don't take it personally.

Use the 'SMILE' structure to help you to increase the success of your calls. You can use it to analyse recorded calls and this will help you to decide what corrective steps you need to take to ensure that all your calls meet professional standards in telephone selling. Figure 5 provides a framework to use. Mark each section of the call and then look at where there is a preponderance of 'no's. This will identify those areas that you need to work on.

Scripted prompts and links

Use these to help you get started. Personalize your prompts so that you are comfortable with what you are saying.

Start with a rapport

'Good morning, Mr Smith, I understand that you are responsible for purchasing stationery for your company, is that correct?'

'Good morning, Mr Smith, my name is Ann Jackson, I'm calling you to discuss our new range of stationery. What stationery do you use in your business?'

'I understand that you use computers, would you tell me a bit more about the consumable products that you use most?'

Maximize the contact

'I'd like to find out more about what influenced your decision to buy from Dicksons and to establish whether our products would be of interest to you. What products will you be buying in the next few weeks?'

'Which is most important to you, Mr Smith, availability of products or after-sales service?'

'What influenced your decision to choose your current product?'

'I appreciate that you may have no immediate requirements, however, you will be reordering at some point in the future, when will that be?'

'If you could change anything about your existing arrangements what would that be?'

Introduce a solution

'From what you have told me, Mr Smith, I believe our new Quadrant range is just what you are looking for because it can give you the flexibility that your customers require.'

'Thank you for that information, Mr Smith, it really does seem that we may be able to help you to improve on your current arrangements. What I would like to suggest is . . .'

'There does seem to be a need for faster delivery times. One of the services we can offer is guaranteed 4-hour delivery. I believe that this would solve your current difficulties.'

'If you could improve the quality of the components you use this would have the effect of increasing the level of satisfaction of your own customers and enable you to gain the improvements in service levels that you are looking for. Our product will help you to do that.'

Look for agreement

'From what you have told me, Mr Smith, I believe our new Quadrant range is just what you are looking for. Do you agree?'

'Does that interest you?'

'When would you like the trial period to start?'

End on a positive note

'I'm pleased that you have decided to go ahead, Mr Smith. I am sure that once you have tried our products you will be glad that you have given us the opportunity to prove to you that we can meet your requirements.'

'I'm delighted that you are interested and I will be happy to supply you with a detailed quotation. When would you like me to call you to progress things further?'

'I'm glad that we have been able to resolve the difficulties that you have been having and that we will continue to do business in the future.'

If the call has not resulted in a sale:

'I'm sorry that we haven't been able to meet your requirements on this occasion. As I mentioned earlier we are constantly looking for ways to offer our customers an improved service. To keep you informed I will contact you next week/month to let you know what we have to offer.'

'I'm sorry that we cannot help you this time, Mr Smith, but I do appreciate the time that you have taken to inform me of your current situation. I would like to call you next month to establish if the situation has changed sufficiently to merit a review of what we have discussed today.'

6 Handling objections over the telephone

In this chapter we will examine further some of the telephone situations that your team are likely to encounter. Handling objections is something salespeople will do possibly many times a day and this skill should be developed so that they are comfortable answering any points that the customer may wish to make during a call. There is no formula for answering objections that guarantees success. However, if you don't attempt to deal with objections when they occur you are guaranteed not to make a sale. The techniques outlined here will help you and your team to develop strategies for handling objections. It may also be necessary to negotiate a satisfactory outcome in which the team feels that it has achieved the best solution for both parties. Negotiation is not simply about price haggling. There are many aspects of a sale that can be negotiated. Concessions must be traded, not 'given away'.

Handling objections

Learn to recognize resistance from your customers. Here are some signs that things are not going well:

- The conversation becomes stilted and you are struggling to maintain momentum.
- The customer's responses are short and unhelpful.
- There is disagreement.
- You find it difficult to establish an area of dissatisfaction – everything in the garden is rosy.
- The customer does not ask you questions that indicate an interest in your proposal.

Sometimes customers will say no to a proposal automatically without really considering their response. It is easier to say no than to say yes. It relieves the customer of the responsibility of making a decision. 'Yes' carries account-ability with it. Customers may say no because it is more comfortable for them to maintain the status quo.

Customers may be inclined to say no if:

- they are new to the position they hold in their company;
- they are timid and indecisive;
- your company has not previously done business with the customer's company;
- your product is new to the market;
- they are worried about the reaction of their external or internal customers;
- they are worried about whether they have negotiated the best terms and conditions;
- they are worried about making the wrong decision;
- they want to avoid making a commitment that may be contractually binding.

It's normal for customers to have concerns; your response must reassure them that they are 'doing the right thing'.

Objections can be described as 'opportunities to sell' or 'requests for more information'. *Learn to love objections!* They are pegs for you to hang your sales hat on. The key to handling objections successfully is:

- know your customers;
- know your market;
- know your company;
- know your product or service;
- know your competition.

Strategies you can use to increase your knowledge and your confidence are:

- talking to customers;
- talking to other people in your company, for example marketing, field sales, managers of other departments;
- reading trade magazines, journals and financial sections in local and national newspapers.

There is no formula stock answer for successfully handling an objection. There are so many variables, your product or service, the customer's needs, the current market climate, competitor activity, etc., that it is not realistic to expect to have one answer that fits all situations. Your strategy can best be summed up as *do something*! Any response is better than silence.

Imagine walking into a high street store. You ask a salesperson to explain the difference between a hi-fi system that costs £500 and one priced £1000. Note that you are not saying that you are unwilling to pay £1000, just that you don't understand the reason for the difference in price. You would be surprised if the salesperson's response was 'Hey, don't ask me, I'm new here. They both look the same to me.' A professional salesperson would seek to establish what a customer needed or wanted from the hi-fi and discuss the reasons for the difference in price. They would draw the customer's attention to the superior features of one model compared to the other. The features would be described in persuasive terms that appeal to the customer based on what the salesperson has learned about the customer's motivation to buy. The customer is then in a position to make an informed decision. If a customer cannot identify a reason for a difference in price then he or she can reasonably conclude that there isn't one and the cheaper price is the better buy. Of course, this may not be true. All products and services are priced differently so a lower price doesn't mean a bargain and a higher price is no guarantee of superior quality. Which is why all price objections should be discussed in terms of *value*.

When customers raise concerns they want answers. If your response is silence then they can only conclude that you agree with them.

Customer: 'That seems expensive. I can get it from another company for much less than that.'
Salesperson: 'Gulp!' [Meta-message: I was wondering when you would say that. I can't think of a single reason why you should buy from us.]

Objections generally tend to centre around one of the following factors:

Your competition

Your competitors are not necessarily offering better value than you are. If your customers are talking to your competitors – they almost certainly are – find out what it is that impresses them and then focus on those areas where you can offer a perceptible difference. Rather than be drawn into a conversation about why your company does not do X, Y or Z, talk about what you can do that your competition cannot do.

The price

If customers bought only the cheapest products and services available there would be only one price for everything! This is not possible because there are so many variables between each product. What are the variables that affect your product price? Value is subjective. Customers may think that the premium price they pay for a designer suit represents good value because of the enhanced prestige they get from wearing a recognizable label. Others may feel that the value is reflected in the quality of the material that is used.

The source

Customers will derive security from dealing with a reputable and successful company. They will be reassured if you tell them about your company's reputation and successes. Tell your customers about the satisfied customers that you have.

From the customer's point of view an objection could occur because the customer does not have sufficient information or has misunderstood the benefits.

Techniques for handling objections

- Listen to customers and allow them to finish what they have to say. If you interrupt you may prevent them from telling you something important.
- Acknowledge the objection. If you pretend that you haven't heard it, it will not go away!
- Appreciate the customer's point of view. Don't rush to the defence of your company.
- Check that you understand the objection.

Before you attempt to answer an objection first qualify it so that you are sure that you have identified the problem correctly.

'Am I right in assuming that it is the price that is the problem?'

Then ask the following question to determine how much the customer is willing to pay:

'You think they are too expensive, may I ask you by how much?'

Then specify the amount the customer quotes.

'So the issue is why should you pay £xxxx more for our product, is that correct Mr/Mrs...?'

Continue:

'If I can justify this price difference will you go ahead?'

If the response from the customer is anything other than a yes then you have not identified the real problem. You will need to question further to find out what the real problem is.

'Something else is concerning you, may I ask what that is?'

Do not attempt to justify your product or service until you have qualified the objection. The customer may be offering an excuse and you could end up answering lots of excuses. The qualifying phrase is:

'If I can ... will you go ahead / place an order?'

Assuming that you have correctly identified the concern you can justify your product or service by using:

- market information;
- facts and figures;
- customer research;
- competitor information;
- testimonials, that is references from satisfied customers;
- case histories;
- articles from trade or professional magazines.

In fact anything that will help you to *paint the picture – tell the story.*

When you are answering objections it is important that you sound at ease and confident. Stay calm and be patient if the customer remains unconvinced. Keep your answers clear and concise. Ensure that the customer is not confused by over-elaborate explanations which miss the point that you want to make. When you have answered the objection confirm that your answer is satisfactory.

'Does that sound reasonable to you?'
'Have I reassured you on that point Mr / Mrs . . .'
'Does that sound fair?'

If the customer's response is 'yes', close the sale.

Strategies for dealing with objections

Do something!

A lost sale is guaranteed if you don't attempt to deal with an objection. Expect customer concerns and experiment with ways to deal with them.

Change your response

If customers challenge your response they are at least interested in understanding your point of view. Once you have convinced them they will probably become your best customers.

Explain the benefits you have discussed

The customers' doubts may be based on a misunderstanding about your product or service. They don't understand what's in it for them. If the customer has no previous experience of your product or service you may have to elaborate benefits which you think are obvious.

Convince customers that they are improving their current arrangements

You have to show enough benefits in the proposition for customers to want to spend their money on what you are offering instead of what they had planned to do. Their motivation to change will be diminished if they do not perceive real advantages over their current practice.

Trust your sales instinct

Listen to what your customers are telling you. If you genuinely put their needs before your own you will know what is right for them and they will trust you to offer the appropriate solution.

Pre-empt customers' objections

You can control the sales conversation by bringing up likely objections (cost etc.) when *you* want to. This approach also deals with an objection before it has a chance to become a serious obstacle.

'I expect that you think all this will prove to be very expensive, so you will be pleased when I tell you that it costs only £xxxx per item. Which is very reasonable, isn't it, Mr/Mrs...?'

Avoid argument

Keep the objection in perspective. Remember that it is a request for information and you will be able to offer a reasonable response. Customers have a right to their point of view.

Let customers finish

Encourage customers to tell you the whole story behind their concern. If you only get half the story you might select the wrong benefits to persuade them.

Question the objection

Be tactful and subtle. Gently question customers' objections to establish *all* the facts. Questioning also allows you to qualify the objection. If customers bombard you with objections it is important to get to the heart of what is really troubling them.

Keep your response short

Going into elaborate and excessive detail will make your customers feel that you are hammering them with unnecessary information. Keep it brief and simple.

Use persuasive words

Use words that have a positive convincing effect on customers. Examples are economical, recommended, genuine, guaranteed, advanced and reputable.

Go digging

Not all objections are voiced. Sometimes you will have to probe for the root cause of a reluctance to buy. Ask questions like:

'What are your main areas of concern?'

Give your customers time to think

Your customer asks for time to think about your proposal and you cannot make any further progress, for example:

Salesperson: 'Are there any particular concerns that I haven't answered, Mr/Mrs...?'
Customer: 'No, I just want time to consider what you have said.'

It may be time to retire from the call and give the customer the opportunity to think about what has been discussed. Most of us do require time to consider making significant purchases and it is appropriate to allow our customers the same courtesy. Sales can be lost because a telephone salesperson hasn't known when to stop. If a customer is giving a proposal serious consideration then progress has been made. Make a telephone appointment to call back at an agreed date and close the sale then.

Scarlett O'Hara

'No' is not a rejection of you personally. A customer may not have the money, need or information to justify buying. This does not mean that you are not a good salesperson. Tomorrow is another day.

Win-Win telephone selling – how to negotiate successfully

Many telephone sales teams have little negotiation power in respect of discounting but even where prices are fixed there is still opportunity to negotiate terms. Customers will ask for other concessions such as free delivery. Some of the aspects of a sale that are negotiable are:

- credit terms;
- delivery charges;
- stockholding;
- volume discounts;
- additional features;
- after-sales service levels.

If you are selling fixed price products or services these aspects present an opportunity to trade concessions with a customer. Any concession that you offer customers must be traded for a concession from them. If this does not happen then the negotiation is 'win-lose'. For example 'free' accessories have a cost attached to them and that cost must be calculated when you are in negotiations, both the cost to your company and the value to your customer. Ideally you want to trade concessions that have more value for the customer than for your company.

To prepare for the start of a negotiation do your homework thoroughly and gather together any facts or figures that may support your position. Take time to familiarize yourself with the customer's priorities. The more you know about customers the more likely it is that you can identify which concessions will appeal to them. Make a statement that indicates that you understand and have considered the customer's point of view. If you are unsure of what customers want ask for information that will explain their position or difficulties. It is more effective to get customers to start the negotiation process by asking them to state what they want. Then you have a good idea of whether the concession that they are seeking is reasonable and whether there is the possibility of common ground between you so that you can reach a mutually acceptable solution. During the negotiation be concise and keep to the point so that the negotiation stays on track. Be prepared to compromise, don't be stubborn, do keep an open mind and search for points that you can concede which can be traded off against the customer's demands. You do not want the negotiation to finish with customers feeling that they have 'lost'. An unhappy customer will look for another supplier.

To negotiate a solution you have to have one. You must take the initiative in choosing the solution otherwise the outcome is more likely to serve your customers' interests only. By offering a solution the negotiation is more likely to centre on reaching agreement and not get stuck in an argument about your refusal to meet customers' terms. When you propose a solution you actually provide useful information to your customers – they do not have to guess what you feel about their suggestion.

Useful questions you can ask are:

'How can we resolve this difficulty?'
'What do you think is an appropriate solution?'
'How does the idea of discussing discounts in return for an increase of orders strike you?'

You can improve your negotiating style by changing the way you talk about yourself. Avoid phrases that put you down. Ask your friends to remind you when you use phrases such as 'It's only me', 'This is probably a silly idea, but', 'I could kick myself' or 'I'm hopeless at...'. Use 'I' when you ask for what you want. Replace statements such as: 'Do you think I could possibly have...' with 'I want...', 'I would like...', 'I need...'.

Here are some suggestions for phrases that you might use during a negotiation of price:

- Prepare your opening statement so that you make an impact and start assertively.

  'Mr/Mrs ... I want you to place your order with my company. Let's see if we can arrive at a solution which is agreeable to both of us.'

- Start by explaining the situation as you see it. Keep to the point and be brief.

  'As I understand it, you want me to offer you a discount on the order that you want to place with me. Is that correct?'

- Acknowledge your own problem but don't blame the customer for it. Empathize with their problems.

'I can appreciate that you want to keep costs to a minimum, however, our products are priced so competitively that to reduce our prices on the basis of a single order would not be a realistic option.'

- Say what you want and offer a compromise if that is possible.

  'If you can increase the level of your commitment by ordering a greater quantity then I think that we can agree a compromise.'

- Outline the benefit for the customer if they accept your terms.

  'That way you can still save money and keep to within your budget.'

- Remind your customer about the value of your product or service.

  'We did agree, didn't we, Mr/Mrs ... that our product was the one that most closely met your requirements, in particular the additional features that will guarantee ease of use.'

Don't take the line of least resistance and do nothing if customers ask for concessions. If you control the conversation and obtain the result that you want you will derive much satisfaction from knowing that you have done your job well, for you and your customer.

Scarlett O'Hara v. Gus Gloom – how to develop a positive attitude towards telephone selling

The secret of sales success is to focus on what you do right and learn how to apply your strengths to any sales situation. All salespeople have to learn to live with failure. It would be nice to think that there is a formula that will guarantee success on every call but unfortunately no such formula exists. Variables out of your control will mean that some calls will not result in a sale. This is not your fault. However, to succeed the maximum number of possible times you will have to make a determined effort to develop your skills and strategies to counteract resistance. If you do not then failure is assured. A little of Scarlett's attitude helps enormously. Tomorrow is another day.

To demonstrate how true it is that a positive attitude affects your sales success, think of those days that you have had which 'start right'. Perhaps a customer that you have been courting for a long time places an order. Great start. The next call you make also ends with an order. Suddenly you can't put a foot wrong – everyone is buying. You are so confident that you make those difficult calls that you have been delaying. Guess what – they buy!

Now consider what happens when you have an 'off' day. The first call yields only a complaint which you cannot resolve satisfactorily. The people around you all appear to be struggling, morale is low. Someone says 'business is bad' or 'no one is buying'. You begin to expect to fail and you do. Nothing has changed except your attitude. If you have days like this do something else. Have a cream cake, take a walk or clean out your desk. Do anything except call your customers, the gloom will only spread to them. Of course, as a telephone sales manager once said to me 'around here you're in the mood whether you're in the mood or not' but a small break can have a positive effect. Don't push your luck though!

You have a right to do business, your product or service can enhance your customers' current arrangements. It is reasonable to want to spread the news. Your time is just as valuable as anyone else's, don't waste it. Talk to people who are interested in what you have to offer. You are the advocate for your company – if you can't think of positive things to say about your company, who can? Use positive words and phrases that will help to persuade your customers and give them confidence in your product or service. For example:

- 'Yes, we can do that for you.'
- 'You will be pleased to know that we have a product that can do exactly that for you.'
- 'We can offer a solution that will solve your difficulties.'

There are some practical things that you can do to counteract negativity:

- Find opportunities, not difficulties.
- Have situations, not problems.
- Have the desire to succeed.
- Welcome objections, and see them as a challenge.
- Reward yourself for achieving your goals.
- Always be looking for new ideas or new business opportunities.

Finally, avoid Gus Gloom. You know the type. When the sun is shining they declare it will rain later, and they carry umbrellas in July. Scarlett is much more fun. So:

- be the sort of person everyone likes to have around;
- surround yourself with positive people.

Here is a typical comment about the change in the consumer and commercial perception of the role of outbound telephone selling in today's business. The speaker was recruited on to a graduate trainee programme before progressing into managing an outbound telephone sales team for the company. The company is highly successful with a multi-billion pound turnover each year.

Its traditional sales approach was entirely face-to-face.

> Over the past five years that I've been involved in outbound telephone calling I have seen a significant change in attitude. When I first started I think the thing that was quite obvious to me, was the fact that when you actually got down to doing the telephone marketing, businesses were very, very receptive but people, internal to the business that you were in, were very a) dubious and b) worried They were initially dubious because they automatically linked telephone marketing activity, regardless of the market and the way in which you went about it and what product you had to offer, as selling double-glazing. The amount of times I heard that was just untrue, and going into it as a career didn't seem like a very good career move to others at the time. When I think about my first job as a telephone sales manager, I met people who I had done a degree with and they perceived it as being a bit of a girl's job, a bit of a backward step, a bit of a cul-de-sac. They thought that it was just running after people on a team and so it didn't seem as though I was doing terribly well for myself. There was no status associated with it at all. When you've got some successes under your belt you can be far more confident and in the early days, although I had a lot of confidence in what we were doing, I couldn't display the results perhaps as quickly as I would have liked to have done. Because it was pioneering, it took some time for the customers to get used to it and for the revenue impact to start to happen. So that is what it was like when I first started up, but within two and half years of start up we proved that it was phenomenally success- ful and we had credibility within the company. Once results were shown and the profitability of contacting customers by phone was proven, we were able to con- vince people at a very senior level. I think that's quite impressive to do in a couple of years, as well as actually doing the day-to-day running of the team to actually change the perception in the company.

(Outbound telephone sales manager)

7 How to enhance telephone performance

Whilst developing the team's sales skills is a priority, other aspects of the job will affect productivity and performance. This chapter focuses on the non-sales aspects of the role. At its simplest, it is no good being the 'best sales-person in the world' if you only call one customer per day. To get results you need both productivity and quality.

Chapter 8 will show you how to enhance the sales performance of the team by analysing the content of the call. This chapter shows you how to improve productivity by exploring the following issues:

- The timing of calls to customers.
- Analysis of your key sales ratios.
- Action planning.

Timing the call

Sales so often fail not because the product or service is wrong but because the timing of the call was wrong. The team may be bashing away on the telephone in a random 'ring as many people as we can' fashion and some sales managers endorse this numbers game: 'The more people you telephone the more sales you will make.' This belief is countered by the quality argument 'Yes, I know my call rate is down but look at the quality of the calls I make. It takes time to develop a good rapport with my customers.' This speaker may be absolutely sincere, and it is a valid argument. However, be prepared for the fact that when you listen to his calls you discover that most of the rapport building is centred on a detailed discussion of the relative merits of a particular holiday resort. One theory is not more correct than the other, nor incorrect for that matter. The truth is that you have to adopt a mixture of the two styles to succeed. If you make *enough calls* and spend *enough time* on them, you will increase your sales. However, a third element, the *timing* of your calls, is just as important and this element of success is often neglected.

It is lovely when you call customers or prospects and they say:

'Gosh, what a coincidence, I was just thinking that I need a new computer with more features, tell me more.'

'Well it's great you have called me, we have been having problems with our current supplier and we want to change.'

'I'm new here and I'm keen to make some changes.'

Responses like these can seem like a ray of sunshine on a cloudy day. They are a good example of why you should telephone your customers instead of waiting for them to telephone you. Of course, not all the people that you call will respond in this manner but you can improve on the 'shotgun' method to increase the number of positive responses that you get by taking a more planned and strategic approach to your outbound calling.

Poor timing leads to a 'not today, thank you' response – crude but effective in quelling even the most enthusiastic salesperson. Typical variations are 'I have all I need for now', 'I've just bought some', 'We've no budget left for that'. Sound familiar? You can avoid this type of response by calling:

- when the customer's stock is low;
- when the customer has had an adequate opportunity to evaluate current practice;
- when the next order is due;
- when the new budget comes into play.

If you don't know the timing of these events, ask your customers, then make a date in your diary (manual or computer) and call them back then. Telephone customers a little before the date they suggest otherwise your competitors may get there before you. It is a question of judgement when you telephone. If it is too soon you may annoy the customer, if it's too late you will have missed an opportunity. A good guideline is to consider the length of the buying cycle. If repurchase takes place every few weeks then a week between calls is sufficient. If the purchase is not to be made for a year then you could let several months go by. Keep calling often enough to maintain a relationship with the customer. If the intervals between each call are too long the customer may be wooed by competitors who are more proactive.

Following up direct mail

It was really strange, my local branch [of a bank] wrote to me offering to conduct a financial review of my affairs. As it happens I am about to get married so I was actually quite interested in what they had to say. The letter said that I would be contacted the following week by someone who would arrange an appointment for me. I never heard from them again. I still don't understand the point of sending me a letter that they had no intention of acting on. I think they must be very disorganized.

Customers and prospects are often 'warmed up' by direct mail that outlines promotions or new products and services that they may be interested in. The major drawback to direct mail is that it is not interactive in the way that a conversation is. It does not allow the customer to ask questions. Therefore the customer must be contacted before the interest stimulated by the direct mail is allowed to fade away. Calling several weeks (in some companies it can be months) after the customer has received the piece will have lower returns than if the customer is called soon after the piece has been received, preferably within the week. The puzzled customer quoted above was unaware that the direct mail piece she had received was part of a programme to increase qualified appointments for her bank's financial advisors. Poor liaison between the people who sent the mailing (marketing) and the people who were supposed to follow it up (the local branch) meant that not only was a business opportunity missed but the customer's perception of the bank was actually diminished. If you make a promise to a customer keep it.

How to create a customer call plan

Call plans are a valuable aid to help your team avoid telephoning the same customers over and over again whilst neglecting others. They will also prevent 'cherrypicking', that is salespeople telephoning the customers they rely on for regular business to the detriment of those who buy less frequently but are none the less important customers to the company. Customers' businesses are dynamic and constantly change. It is essential to keep up with the changes so that any opportunities to do business are not lost. Telephoning favourite customers is rewarding because the relationship between them and your company is warm but if the rest of the customer base is neglected you will lose the opportunity to grow the business. If you know that some customers are neglected or that the team never has time for prospecting, a call plan will help you get the team organized. Segment your customer base and decide on the call frequency. A simple rule is the more the customer spends with your company the closer you get to the customer!

You can segment by the amount customers spend with you, the frequency that they order or their potential spending with the company should you persuade them to use you as their sole supplier. Figure 6 provides an example of how you might arrange your call cycle for existing customers.

The territory consists of 200 customers who have been segmented as follows:		
Number of customers	**Amount spent p.a.**	**Minimum call frequency**
20	£10 000	1 call per week
50	£5000	1 call per two weeks
30	£1000	1 call per month
100	£500	1 call per quarter

Figure 6   Call cycle

Now add up how many effective calls you need to make per annum to achieve adequate coverage of your territory. Multiply the number of customers by the number of calls required per annum (Figure 7). Assume a working year of 42 weeks to take into account the weeks that a salesperson is likely to be unavailable, for example holidays, training, etc. You can adjust this figure to the requirements of your own organization.

Number of customers	**Effective calls needed per annum**	**Total effective calls per annum per customer segment**
20	50	1000
50	25	1250
30	12	360
100	4	400
Total effective calls per annum		3010

Figure 7   Call plan

You can now calculate how many effective calls you need to make per day by using the following method:

$$\frac{\text{total no. of calls per annum}}{\text{available weeks}} \div \text{working days in a week} = \text{effective calls per day}$$

Thus

$$\frac{3010}{42} \div 5 = 14.3$$

The call cycle should be set at an appropriate rate for your business. In some companies, the customer will be called every day, in others the frequency may be much less. Your average length of call may be a few minutes or be much longer and this will affect how many calls you make. You can adjust the methodology above to calculate the effective daily call rate for your own sales territory. The important point is to ensure that your customers are telephoned frequently enough to avoid the possibility of losing their loyalty and custom.

If we assume a calls/effective contact ratio of 2:1 then you will require a call rate of 29 outbound calls per day in the example above. If the calls to effective contact ratio is higher, then your call rate target will be higher, for example a 3:1 rate will require 43 calls per day. Of course, this does not take into account any other telephone activity that you may have, such as prospecting, mailshot follow ups, etc., which will usually require more calls to achieve an effective contact. You may need to identify the calls/effective contact ratio separately for each call type. If we assume that the average length of a call in the example is 5 minutes then a salesperson would be actively using the telephone for an average of 2.41 hours per day. This may be appropriate for someone who has lots of administration to do but leaves someone with little administration ample time to engage in other telephone activities whilst still managing existing customers effectively. Use a time log (Figure 8) to calculate the time your team has available for telephone calling. It will help you to identify what time is spent on non-sales tasks. If your salespeople have more time than they need to call all their customers in the contact plan, they can fill the gap with prospect calls etc. If there is no gap you might consider reducing the size of the sales territory to accommodate prospecting or delegating prospecting or non-sales tasks to others in the team. Write a realistic achievable plan which the salesperson will stick to rather than one that does not accurately reflect work practice.

How to analyse results

An interesting question is 'How many calls do you have to make to make a sale?' If a fog descends at this point this section will help you to lift it. To make an informed decision about who and when to telephone, you need reliable statistics on which to base your decisions. Telephone sales information is easy to acquire and collate. You can collect data even if you don't have sophisticated computers to help you.

Key telephone sales ratios

First of all, what do you want to measure? Ideally you will want qualitative

Name:	Date:

Time	Details
8.00	
8.30	
9.00	
9.30	
10.00	
10.30	
11.00	
11.30	
12.00	
12.30	
1.00	
1.30	
2.00	
2.30	
3.00	
3.30	
4.00	
4.30	
5.00	
5.30	

Figure 8   Time log

and quantitative information. You need to measure quality (i.e. the content of the call) and productivity. Success is not achieved by merely increasing productivity nor is it just about finely honed sales skills. Professional telephone selling is a successful combination of the two. To prioritize your calls and invest in the telephone activity that brings you the greatest return, you will need to measure the outcome of the call. Whether your information is collected via the computer or manually is not important, it is collecting and *using* the information that counts.

Your information can be divided into three categories:

- The number of calls that are made.
- The type of calls that are made.
- The outcome of the calls.

The number of calls that are made

To assess whether someone is performing to the appropriate level of productivity an average of the team's call rate can be used as a benchmark. If productivity falls below the minimum accepted standard it is usually an indicator of a problem such as demotivation, too much administration, too large a sales territory, etc. which will have to be addressed. Call statistics from your telephone system will provide you with detailed information. For a small fee you can get management information from your telecoms provider which will show how many calls are made, whether they are incoming or outgoing, when the calls are made and how long each call lasts. You can easily identify peaks and troughs in call traffic. You will probably discover some surprising information:

- Your team spends less time on the telephone than you thought.
- The calls aren't as long as you thought.
- It takes a long time to work up to the first call of the day.

All of which is food for thought.

The type of calls that are made

Knowing the type of calls that are made will enable you to focus your team's sales activities on the calls that bring the most return for effort. It is reasonable to assume that calling existing customers is more likely to be successful because of the relationship that is already established than calling people with whom you have had no contact, that is cold-calling. Between these two extremes there are a number of possibilities that you should consider. For example does calling someone who has received a direct mail piece yield more sales than calling someone who has not and, if so, how does the ratio of calls to sales compare? Other questions you might want to ask include the following:

- Does a care calling programme yield more business than if you didn't have one?

- How does the number of orders that are placed when you follow up quotations compare to not following up quotations?
- How much time do you spend on handling incoming calls which prevent you from actively calling to stimulate new or additional business?
- How many calls are to customers who have queries that result in the need for your assistance?
- How successful are your diaried calls compared to unplanned calls?
- Does cleaning your mailing list improve the number and quality of responses that you get?

Collect information that will give you data on the following:

- List cleaning.
- Direct mail calls.
- Prospect calls.
- Calls to existing customers.
- Calls in response to customer queries or requests for information.
- Care calls as part of your account management programme.
- Calls to follow up quotations.
- Diaried callbacks.
- Calls to promote specific promotions that your company may be running.
- Calls to follow up referrals that you have been given by customers.

When you know the numbers you can start to crunch them!

The outcome of the calls

What happened, did you . . .

- get through to a decision-maker;
- conduct a fact find;
- get through to someone who influences the decision;
- close a sale;
- make an appointment;
- prepare a quotation;
- diary a callback when the customer will be willing to speak to you again;
- cross-sell or up-sell;
- continue to negotiate;
- decide not to pursue further (knowing when to accept rejection is as important a skill as knowing when to pursue a sale).

Calls that do not result in a sale are not failures. If you have moved along the continuum towards a sale you will have made progress.

Now you are ready to produce some interesting facts and figures. Key performance indicators are:

- no. of calls to effective contacts;
- no. of quotations to effective contacts;
- no. of quotations to sale.

Each set of statistics can be tracked back to the type of call to enable you to decide which calls produce the most results. This information will also improve your sales forecasting. Crystal balls and wishful thinking don't cut much ice with sales and marketing directors. If there are no 'warmed' leads for you to call you can reflect this in your forecast by using sales ratios for cold-calling. This will allow your forecasts to be more accurate.

Knowledge of these ratios will enable you to develop a strategy to help you to achieve your targets and improve your performance. Assuming that the remedy is to increase productivity is too simplistic. You are more likely to be successful if you set specific targets. Be precise about where an increase in productivity will yield the best results. Look for those areas where an increase in sales skills is required rather than more calls.

Look at the sales ratios in Figure 9. What do they tell you?

Strategy for Salesperson A

The first priority is for this salesperson to increase the average value of order. If she achieves an average value of £50 like Salesperson B she will achieve revenue of £10 000 which will put her right back on target. If she also achieves Salesperson B's effective call to sale ratio this would yield an extra £3300 per month which would put her over target and into favour with her manager.

Strategy for Salesperson B

On the face of it Salesperson B is doing fine but a closer examination of the figures show that he is not as effective at getting through to decision-makers as his colleagues A and C. If B achieved a similar ratio of speaking to one in every two decision-makers he telephoned, he would yield an extra three sales per day, be £3000 over target and have a very happy sales manager. B could go from a target achiever to a target buster and star material.

Salesperson A has a target of £10 000 revenue per month to achieve. Currently achieving £8000 per month.*

No. of calls per day:	40
No. of contacts per day:	20
No. of sales per day:	10
Average value of order	£40

Salesperson B has a target of £10 000 revenue per month to achieve. Currently achieving £10 000 per month.

No. of calls per day:	40
No. of contacts per day:	15
No. of sales per day:	10
Average value of order	£50

Salesperson C has a target of £10 000 revenue per month to achieve. Currently achieving £3500 per month.

No. of calls per day:	30
No. of contacts per day:	15
No. of sales per day:	5
Average value of order	£35

The key sales ratios are:

Ratios analysed	Salesperson A	Salesperson B	Salesperson C
Number of calls	40	40	30
Calls to effective contacts	2 : 1	2.7 : 1	2 : 1
Effective contacts to orders	2 : 1	1.5 : 1	3 : 1
Average value of order	£40	£50	£35

* Assumes five working days a week, four weeks a month.

Figure 9   Sales ratios

Strategy for Salesperson C

Oh dear, quite a bit to do here. The immediate priority for C is to increase her productivity. An extra 10 calls per day would yield an extra sale per day. This would increase her revenue total to £4 200 without any improvement in sales skills. C sells to one in every three people that she speaks to, and if this could be increased to the 2:1 achieved by A it would yield an extra five sales per day (assuming 40 calls) and a revenue of £7000. Finally she could focus on increasing the average value of an order. So C's action plan would be:

1   Increase calls by 10 per day.
2   Increase sales to effective contact ratio to 2:1.
3   Increase average value of order.

Point 2 indicates that C would benefit from further training on closing the sale. Further areas for development would be revealed by listening closely to C's calls and identifying more specific training needs.

Careful analysis of your team's call activity and results will enable you to adopt strategies that will get the team back on target and will help team members to avoid that uncertain 'what do I do now' feeling. Just knowing what they need to do will boost their confidence and put them back on track.

Action planning

From the information you have gained from analysing your key sales ratios and your competence assessment sheets (which are discussed in Chapter 8), you will now have a much clearer idea of the changes needed to increase your team's sales performance. You can pull this information together and make it easier to manage by formalizing it into an action plan (Figure 10 overleaf). This will help you to measure progress and keep on track.

When you write an action plan prioritize your sales objectives and put them into a time frame. They should be subject to regular review. This review may be formal, that is, with you, or used as a tool by a team member to ensure effective self-management of call activities. It is important to set realistic and specific objectives. 'To make more calls' is vague and unhelpful. It is more effective to say 'I will make an average of 10 more calls per day in the next month.' Because it will take time to achieve the required level of activity, specify an average so that by the end of the month the overall objective can be achieved even if there have been fluctuations on a daily basis. Base your increases on incremental steps. A leap from say 20 calls per day to 80 calls per day would be unrealistic for your salespeople. Action plans can be rewritten as needed. If you have been over-ambitious you can set more realistic goals when you have had the opportunity to assess the team's progress.

Objective	Action	Time frame for achievement of objective
To increase productivity	Make 10 more calls per day	One month
To conduct desk research that will yield more prospects	To spend a minimum of two hours per week researching	One month
To consolidate relation-ships with key customers	Arrange customer visits to site (minimum of four visits)	Two months
To increase profit per order	To undertake training in negotiation	To be completed in next six weeks

Date agreed:

Signature of sales executive:

Signature of coach:

Comments:

Review date:

Figure 10   Action plan

8 How to use tape recordings to assess competence

Competence assessment checklist

How competent salespeople are on the telephone cannot be assessed accurately unless there is an opportunity to listen to their calls and to monitor what happens during them. The assessment needs to be as objective as possible. Some areas will necessarily be subjective, for example whether the telephone salesperson sounds 'friendly'. Recording the calls so that relevant parts of the tape can be played back to support your assessment is useful. A checklist that incorporates the sales skills that you want to assess will help to standardize the process so that everyone is assessed in the same manner using the same criteria. Figure 11 is an example of a typical assessment checklist and the format allows you to substitute or add any criteria you wish. If you decide to create your own competence assessment checklist the criteria should reflect the structure of the sale and the objectives of the call. Alternatively you can use the 'SMILE' checklist in Chapter 5 (Figure 5).

Tape analysis

Recordings of live calls will give you the opportunity to analyse what happens during a call. Telephone selling requires the ability to maintain the direction and flow of a conversation and sometimes the ability to think quickly. Everyone wishes that they had the benefit of hindsight and listening to calls will help your team to develop sales strategies for future calls. Debriefing is limited if you can only refer to what you have heard in a call with no recording to confirm what the individuals said. Even if notes are made your recollection and that of the salesperson will differ. A subjective opinion, for example whether the tone of voice was warm and friendly, is

Telephone skills	Yes	No
Opening/introduction		
Confirms contact is decision-maker		
Name is offered		
Reason for call is stated		
Uses customer's name		
Content of the call		
Asks appropriate questions		
Establishes need for product/service		
Confirms customer's requirements		
Uses relevant benefits		
Surrounds price with benefits		
Gains commitment		
Asks for the order		
Range sells where appropriate		
Confirms order		
Objections		
Clarifies objection		
Answers objection		
Confirms that the customer agrees		
Telephone skills		
Uses positive language		
Listens actively		
Sounds confident		
Sounds friendly		
Voice is clear and articulate		
Allows customer to finish before speaking		
Action points		

Figure 11   Assessment checklist

accepted if salespeople can hear for themselves how they sound to customers. Hearing recordings of live calls can be revelatory to salespeople who will often need no more than the opportunity to listen to recordings to identify their strengths and weaknesses. When salespeople analyse a recording of a call they are generally too hard on themselves and some positive feedback from you or their colleagues will be required to put their reaction into perspective.

Using a tape recorder will also allow you to rewind and listen again to important segments of the call. This will give you time to really think about possible alternative responses. What follows are some transcriptions of real calls. Identifying names have been removed for the sake of confidentiality. Literal transcriptions of the spoken word reveal that salespeople speak using a verbal shorthand to emphasize certain points. Read aloud these transcripts and see how they differ to the image that they create in print. What looks incomprehensible in writing may make perfect sense when spoken.

Example 1

The first transcript is from a call to an existing customer following the mailing of a catalogue. It is worth noting that the catalogue was comprehensive and included an enormous range of products that the company could supply. It was expensive to produce and featured new products not previously supplied by the company.

The objectives of this call were to establish:

- what products the customer might be interested in;
- what if any health and safety products the customer currently purchased;
- when the customer would be purchasing similar products again; and
- whether the customer's reaction to the new catalogue was positive.

Therefore preplanned questions could have been:

'Can you tell me what products appealed to you the most?'
'What health and safety products do you currently purchase?'
'When will you be ordering products?'
'Please tell me what you liked best about the new products in our new catalogue?'

Let's examine the content of the call in more detail to see where the salesperson could improve his sales technique.

Speaker	Analysis
Salesperson: 'Oh good afternoon Mrs . . . my name is . . . calling from [names company]. This is just a quick call – do you have a couple of moments to spare?'	Whilst it is polite to ask a customer if she is free to take the call try to avoid inviting a negative reaction to the call. 'This is just a quick call' demeans the call for both parties. The metamessage is 'My time is not as important as yours.'
Customer: 'Yes.' *Salesperson:* 'Thanks. It's in relation to the catalogue that we sent recently. At the moment what we are trying to do is gauge the reaction to the catalogue and obviously find out if you are happy receiving it. Did you get a copy yourself?'	After the purpose of the call has been stated engage the customer's attention and participation in the conversation. Begin with 'I would like to discuss . . . with you' or 'I am interested in your opinion about our new catalogue, please tell me...? 'Did you get a copy yourself?' will nearly always elicit a no or the response which was actually given by the customer in this conversation.
Customer: 'I have actually but I haven't had a chance to look at it yet, but I have received it.' *Salesperson:* 'OK, would you prefer it if I called you back at a later date when you've had a chance to look through it? See if you have any questions or queries?'	The salesperson feels that he has nowhere to go with the call other than an offer to call back when the customer has read the catalogue. The catalogue is on the desk, the contact is on the telephone – make the most of this opportunity by involving the customer with 'That's great. What I would like to do is to refer you to page . . . where our new products are featured. Tell me, what you think of them?' If you prefer to call back, the phrase 'questions or queries' indicates that the caller is not expecting a positive response from the customer. It would be more positive to say 'We are really interested in your comments on our new catalogue. When can I call you to discuss your reaction?'
Customer: 'I have had a quick flick through.'	If the opening question had not been closed this might have been revealed earlier.
Salesperson: 'Any idea how you find the product range?'	This question is clumsily phrased because not enough preplanning has gone into the call.
Customer: [speaks – reply unclear] *Salesperson:* 'Oh, yes?' *Customer:* 'So, er, you know, products that, uhm, that, uhm, or companies that supply software products.'	

Speaker	**Analysis**
Salesperson: 'Oh, I see.'	
Customer: 'Uhm, to help you, uhm, to like manage your system really, rather than specific products, as in hardware products.'	This would be a good time to summarize what you think the customer is looking for. The customer appears to be confused so leading the conversation will help her to articulate her thoughts more clearly. Try 'Would I be right in saying that you are interested in buying a software program that will enable you to manage health and safety issues more effectively?'
Salesperson: 'Did you find anything of interest?'	The salesperson is asking the customer to identify her own needs. This is the salesperson's job. Control of the call is handed over to the customer. If the salesperson knew the contents of the catalogue better he would have been able to suggest a solution.
Customer: 'I didn't actually, no. I didn't actually find any software products in there, I don't think.'	
Salesperson: 'Oh, OK.	The salesperson could have given more specific help here: 'You will find the products that you are looking for on page . . .'
Customer: 'I'm not sure whether there are any, but I only had a quick look through.'	
Salesperson: 'So it's software solely that you are interested in?'	The salesperson has assumed this without adequate questioning. Again there is no direct response to the customer's comment that she could not find what she wanted in the catalogue. The salesperson could have learned more about what health and safety issues were important to the customer.
Customer: 'Really, yeah, to help manage it really.'	
Salesperson: 'Right.'	
Customer: 'To do with office safety, management of hazardous substances and those kind of things.'	
Salesperson: 'Have you had a look at the section with all the books and videos in. Is that any use at all?'	The subject of managing dangerous substances could have been explored further. Sales opportunities could have been present for selling protective clothing and other associated products.
Customer: 'I did have a look through there yeah, uhm . . .'	
Salesperson: 'I mean looking through it here there are absolutely loads to	If there are no 'software' products in the catalogue it is clear that the salesperson is

Speaker	Analysis
choose from but obviously it's only specifically software you are interested in. I'll tell you what I'll do I'll give you – this is to help you – I'll give you our helpline number.' [Gives number]	trying to direct the customer to alternative sources of information at the back of the catalogue. However, by saying 'obviously it's only specifically software you are interested in' the salesperson is actually reducing the possibility of stimulating the customer's interest in other products.
Salesperson: 'Uhm, is there anything else I can help you with while I'm on the phone?' *Customer:* 'No, there isn't at the moment, no.' *Salesperson:* 'I see, well feel free to give us a ring if you ever need any help or assistance. Obviously we have given you the helpline number so hopefully they will be a source of information to you as well.' *Customer:* 'Yes, I will give them a ring.' *Salesperson:* 'OK, Mrs . . . Thanks very much for your time.' *Customer:* 'Thanks very much.'	Again the customer is encouraged to lead the call. The question is closed and invites a 'no'. Which is what the salesperson gets. The call ends with no indication given to the customer when she can expect another call. With such a variety of products available in the catalogue the salesperson is over-relying on the catalogue to sell rather than actively looking for the sales needs and matching them. The offer of an alternative source of information is helpful but the primary role of the salesperson is to sell. Sales opportunities have not been maximized on this call.

Example 2

The segment below is taken from a call made to a customer who uses more than one supplier. The company calling is not the customer's main supplier and the salesperson is aware of the strong competition from local suppliers who trim margins to win business. The company finds it difficult to compete on price but can offer the customer well stocked warehouses which means immediate delivery. The customer tends to use the company only if he cannot source cheaper items locally. The company has an outbound team to help it generate business but the team has the disadvantage that because the company's computer systems don't talk to each other there is little accurate information on customers who may be buying from it. This segment starts after the introduction.

Speaker	**Analysis**
Salesperson: 'So how often do you purchase from us, is it weekly or monthly or what?'	The sales information available to the salesperson is limited due to incompatible computer systems but rather than advertise the fact to the customer it would be preferable to say 'How frequently do you purchase from us compared to your other suppliers Mr . . .?'
Customer: 'Well, daily. It depends on what people want you see. It can be daily you know.'	
Salesperson: 'Have you got anything hanging around now?'	I feel another 'or what' hanging in the air! Not surprisingly the customer is puzzled by this question.
Customer: 'What stuff, you mean your stuff?'	
Salesperson: 'No, I mean orders.'	If you mean orders say so, hedging the question will only confuse the customer. Try 'What will you be ordering today?'

Example 3

The next call was made by a member of an outbound telephone sales team which supports the activities of field sales account managers. In this instance negotiations had taken place between the field sales account manager and the company's head office. The telephone salesperson was following up the negotiations currently taking place with direct calls to the sites which belonged to the parent company. This was to ensure that all sales opportunities were maximized locally as well as nationally. The product details have been changed to conceal the company's identity otherwise the call is a literal transcript. The call begins as the salesperson is connected.

Speaker	**Analysis**
Customer: 'Andrew Smith.'	
Salesperson: 'Good morning, Andy, it's Mark calling from [gives company name].'	The customer's response indicates a preference to be called Andrew. The salesperson presumes that the customer will not object to the familiar 'Andy'. It will be easier to establish a rapport with the customer if these verbal clues are noticed by the salesperson.
Customer: 'Yes.'	
Salesperson: 'Hello, how are you?'	Cliché questions will elicit cliché responses.
Customer: 'All right, thank you.	

Speaker	**Analysis**
Salesperson: 'Good, good. I'm calling regarding some information we've been sending out to all of the sites regarding a special offer on PCs. Have you received that at all?'	It is best to start the call with an assumption that the customer has received the information. If you ask a customer if they have received information almost invariably the response will be no. Try 'I sent you some information, I would like to know what you think of the special offer?' If the customer hasn't read the information this question may at least stimulate some interest in the special offer.
Customer: 'You're sending it out to all the sites?'	
Salesperson: 'That's right.'	
Customer: 'Er, no.'	
Salesperson: 'It's a special offer we've put together especially for all the XXX Group.'	
Customer: 'Is that the one, is that the one, just a minute, is that the one from Patrick Small?'	
Salesperson: 'Patrick Small? Oh right, so have you spoken to him?'	
Customer: 'Yes.'	
Salesperson: 'You have, right OK.'	
Customer: 'What's the special offer you're putting together?'	
Salesperson: 'It's exactly the same as Patrick's. I think he has already spoken to you.'	
Customer: 'Well, I've been chasing Patrick now for a month to get me some figures and I've been speaking to Chris O'Farrell as well.'	
Salesperson: 'Right.'	Some acknowledgement of the customer's problems in getting the figures that he requires is needed here other than 'right'.
Customer: 'I've got a meeting with Patrick at the end of this month but he's faxing me some figures through this morning.'	
Salesperson: 'Right.'	
Customer: 'But if that's the best you can come up with I shan't be using you.'	
Salesperson: 'Was that the 486 PC or the one with the docking system?'	The salesperson is avoiding the issue. The customer is clearly unhappy with the quotation but gets no response to the comment 'if that's the best you can come up with I shan't be using you'. Avoidance can be effective at deflecting comments that are not serious reservations but if the

Speaker	Analysis
	customer repeats the reservation then it is more than likely a real objection not just an excuse.
Customer: 'Er, just have a look again, yes.' *Salesperson:* 'Right.' *Customer:* 'The 486 PC or the one with the docking system?' *Salesperson:* 'Yes, that's right.' *Customer:* 'Does that include business software?' *Salesperson:* 'Yes, that's free of charge. Is that the same offer you've got?' *Customer:* 'Er, that's the same one I've got yes.' *Salesperson:* 'Yes.' *Customer:* 'Software free of charge, installation £50.' *Salesperson:* 'Right.'	'Right' seems to be a standard response no matter what the customer says! Try to vary your responses or the customer will think that you are not really interested in what they are saying.
Customer: 'What does the installation include?' *Salesperson:* 'Erm . . .'	The salesperson needs to understand his product and service fully to retain credibility with the customer. 'Erm' doesn't do it.
Customer: 'Will the PC be ready to use?' *Salesperson:* 'I would assume that it will be.'	The salesperson is struggling with will it or won't it be ready to use. Assumptions are not convincing. This response underlines the importance of sound product training.
Customer: 'Then you've got an installation of £50.' *Salesperson:* 'Right.' *Customer:* 'I can't, I can't weigh that up.' *Salesperson:* 'Right, what the £50?' *Customer:* 'Yes.' *Salesperson:* 'OK, is that the, is that the thing that is putting you off the offer?'	This is a good attempt to qualify the objection. Before attempting to respond to customers' concerns it is important to identify any other points that may be bothering them. The qualification works as this customer's next statement shows. There are indeed other things that will influence the customer's buying decision.

Speaker

Customer: 'Well, it's not only that, it's your monthly maintenance charge of £20, erm, I'm dealing on £15 a month with Bloggs and Co., including call out and labour.'
Salesperson: 'Yes, no call out charge, it's the same with us.'
Customer: 'Yes, but yours is £20 a month.'
Salesperson: '£20 a month?'
Customer: 'Yes, the maintenance is £20.'
Salesperson: 'Right. OK, because I could probably get a 5 per cent discount on the maintenance.'

Customer: 'Yes, well, it's 5 per cent, it's only going to bring it to £19 only, yes, and with Bloggs you get full cover. Bloggs is still giving us more you see.'
Salesperson: 'Right, OK.'
Customer: 'I get full cover and I'm only paying £15 and Chris said to me yesterday Patrick was going to give me an offer I couldn't refuse.'
Salesperson: 'Right, OK.'
Customer: 'So if that's the best offer, erm, it's no good to me.'
Salesperson: 'Right, OK, what I'll do is, I'll get in touch with Patrick myself then and see what he has to say and I'll pass on all the information that you have given me as well.'
Customer: 'That's it, well, I'm querying that £50.'
Salesperson: 'Er, yes, the installation.'
Customer: 'Installation.'
Salesperson: 'Yes.'
Customer: 'But you know, well, it needs more serious thought.'

Analysis

The salesperson could try a number of tactics before offering a discount. To move straight to a discount price will convince the customer that his assertion is correct, that is that the service is too expensive. The salesperson could find out more about what the customer was getting from the salesperson's competitor. What are the significant points of difference? Guaranteed response times for example. The customer is very forthcoming about the price difference. Use this information to qualify the objection: 'If I could justify that extra £5 per month would you go ahead?'

The buck is passed. Let Patrick take care of it.

Speaker	Analysis
Salesperson: 'Yes, OK, then.'	This salesperson has now given up. His response does nothing to lead the customer away from the reservations and into a problem-solving conversation. Try 'I appreciate that you want to think it over. It is an important decision. Whoever you choose will have to be reliable. Our pricing for installation and maintenance reflects the expertise and reliability of our people. What would happen if your contractor proved to be unreliable?'
Customer: 'All right?' *Salesperson:* 'What I'll do now is I'll see if I can get hold of Patrick and I'll give you a call back.'	The inference here is that the salesperson is going to ask Patrick to reduce the price to match what the customer has been quoted. This may not be possible nor is it desirable. The service is priced competitively. Companies rarely price themselves out of the market as a deliberate strategy. The salesperson needs to justify the price not match it. If the price cannot be reduced where is the salesperson to go? He has undermined his position by seeming to agree with everything that the customer has said. Further if a callback is suggested the message must be clear. Say when you are calling back, be specific.
Customer: 'OK.' *Salesperson:* 'OK.' *Customer:* 'Cheers.' *Salesperson:* 'Thanks, bye.' *Customer:* 'Bye.'	

Example 4

This next call is made to an existing customer as part of a company's care call programme. The salesperson has chosen to approach the call as a survey into the customer's attitude towards the company and hopes to establish (a) that the customer is satisfied with the level of service that he is getting and (b) to introduce the customer to some discounts to which he is entitled.

Speaker	Analysis
Salesperson: 'Oh, good morning, could I speak to Mr Johnson please?' *1st contact:* 'Ah, sorry.'	

Speaker	Analysis
Salesperson: 'My name's Liz Brown. I'm calling from XYZ company.'	
1st contact: 'Right, I'll try and put you through to reception. You've come through on a very strange line. You've come through on a direct line rather than our main line.'	
Salesperson: 'Oh, right, I beg your pardon.'	
1st contact: 'Just one moment please.'	
[pause]	
Customer: 'Can I help?'	
Salesperson: 'Oh, hello there, er, yes my name's Liz Brown calling from XYZ, erm, I've been asked by your account manager to call around just to basically do a survey of, er, you know what, er, you'd use at the moment, you know . . . we have customer service levels that sort of thing.'	At this point the salesperson has no idea who she is talking to but she presses on thinking that she has got through to the person that she asked to speak to. It is always advisable to confirm who you are speaking to before you begin the conversation. Try 'Thank you, can I confirm that I am speaking to Mr Johnson?'
	Call preplanning could have got the salesperson off to a much more positive start. Try 'Our account manager has asked me to call you to establish what equipment you are using on this site. Can you tell me what you have there?'
Customer: 'Oh, right. Who told you to actually call Mr Johnson?'	
Salesperson: 'Er, that's just the contact name that we have on this list that we have, sorry.'	'That's just the contact name' does not reflect the importance of the contact to the customer's company. The metamessage is 'I've got to speak to someone and he will do.'
Customer: 'Right.'	
Salesperson: 'So it's possible . . .'	
Customer: [interrupts] 'I think it would be a good idea to take that one off.'	
Salesperson: 'Oh, right, OK.'	
Customer: 'I don't think he'd appreciate it if he gets called for a survey.'	This is the result you get if you diminish the purpose of your call to a 'survey' or 'customer service levels sort of thing' at the outset of the call. The speaker feels that such a call is not important enough for Mr Johnson to take.
Salesperson: 'Oh, I see. OK, right, yes so, erm, I just wondered whether there's any issues that you know you would like XYZ to improve upon? If you can call to mind at all?'	The hesitant approach to the subject demonstrates that the salesperson feels uncomfortable about receiving a reply that may be too difficult for her to handle. It does not instil confidence in the customer. Be specific. Try 'What issues are

Speaker	Analysis
	important to you Mr . . . how can we help you to improve your current arrangements?' Before asking for the customer's opinion it would be sensible to establish who the customer is! You need to know the source of an opinion.

Customer: 'Price.'
Salesperson: 'Right. Is that . . . er . . .'
Customer: 'That's the basic issue. You tell your account manager . . . this is XYZ account manager?'
Salesperson: 'That's right, yes.'
Customer: 'Right, erm, it's just that really these decisions aren't made from this office, they're made from head office.'
Salesperson: 'Right, erm, because you mentioned price, we've just got a couple of discounts you might be interested in actually, erm, one would be on the maintenance of the equipment that you have down there.'

The salesperson has not heard the latter comment only the fact that the customer has expressed a concern about price. Reaction to the mention of price is to talk immediately about 'discounts'. The salesperson would benefit from further exploration of the customer's comment 'decisions aren't made from this office, they're made from head office'. If such decisions are centralized then it is not appropriate to pursue the subject of discounts on this call. It would be more helpful to the salesperson to ask questions to find out what the role of the customer is and how the customer fits in with the company's purchasing and decision-making structure.

Customer: 'Right.'
Salesperson: 'Erm, how long would you be contemplating keeping that equipment on?'
Customer: 'The foreseeable future really, I don't think we've got any plans to change it. We've probably had it three years.'
Salesperson: 'Oh right, I see this and this works fine during that time then?'
Customer: 'We've had no problems.'
Salesperson: 'Right, we can give you about 15 per cent off the maintenance charges for that, erm, as long as you have it over a five-year period.'

The hesitancy over the introduction of the condition of a five-year contract period betrays the uncertainty of the salesperson as to how he believes customers will react to this condition. Be positive. Try 'We can offer significant savings if you use our equipment for a limited period of five years.'

Speaker

Customer: 'Right so . . .'
Salesperson: 'If you were to upgrade it you know to another XYZ system then, of course, we'd just migrate it over to that.'
Customer: 'Right.'
Salesperson: 'Or if you were to move, just take it with you.'
Customer: 'I see, right, so do you have details that you can send?'

Salesperson: 'I do indeed, yes, I'd be more than happy to send some figures through to you, erm, can I take your fax number?'

Customer: 'Yes, it's [gives number].'
Salesperson: [repeats number] 'Right, OK, and on the subject of, er, saving money I've also noticed that we might be able to give you some money off other items as well. We have a discount package called ABC for all your equipment called . . .'
Customer: [interrupts] 'Had that one, yes.'
Salesperson: 'Yes, and we've improved it recently, er, you know with all the XYZ discounts going on at the moment I'm sure you know there's a price war out there. And what we're offering is up to 20 per cent discount for . . .'

Customer: 'Hm, hm.'
Salesperson: 'and possibly up to 27 per cent on certain items.'
Customer: 'Right. Which is quite good I'm sure but, erm, I just think that kind of decision isn't made from here.'

Analysis

The use of the word 'migrate' is confusing. Try 'If you purchase another system during this period we can transfer your agreement to new equipment.'

This response needs to be clarified. Are decisions made on this site and the customer has been misdirecting the salesperson or is the customer asking for details as a quick way to end the call? Ask the customer if he is interested.

Sending 'figures' takes time and costs money. If the salesperson makes this commitment then she should seek information about the process. Who is considering the figures? When will a decision be made? Does the customer want the figures to be sent by fax? Is the decision to be made within hours or weeks? Remember that figures alone do not sell, the customer needs to understand the benefits.

'With all the XYZ discounts going on at the moment' and 'a price war out there' are both comments that should be avoided at all costs! The customer may not have been aware of or has not received some of the discounts referred to. The salesperson's company may indeed be in a price war but it is more discreet to keep this information to yourself.

This is the second time that the salesperson has been given this information. Now an attempt has to be made to find out more about how the decision-making

Speaker

Analysis

process works in this company. If the speaker does not make the decision, who does? Calls can still be productive if they move you along the sales continuum. The salesperson may not be speaking to a decision-maker but she is speaking to someone who can at least point her in the right direction. Perhaps Mr Johnson could help after all?

Salesperson: 'Right.'
Customer: 'So we have a group agreement for our company at the moment and we abide by that.'
Salesperson: 'Right, OK. No problem at all. But in the meantime I'll fax you the things for your own maintenance that's just on-site.'
Customer: 'Right.'
Salesperson: 'So there's savings to be made there you know and if you're quite happy with the system then, er, it would be quite good to take up.'
Customer: 'Yes.'
Salesperson: 'Can I take your name, please?'

Oh dear!

At last! The position held in the company by the speaker should also be checked. Conversations always flow much easier if you know who you are talking to and you can use the customer's name during the call.

Customer: 'It's [gives name].'
Salesperson: 'Right. OK [name], er, if you leave that with me I'll get these prices faxed to you and I'll leave my contact details on there, you know, in case you wish to take that one up.'

If the customer does not 'wish to take that one up' what action is the salesperson going to take? Quotations are not worth sending out if they are not followed up by a telephone call in *every* case. Try 'I will call you back with the figures and we can discuss this further.' If the figures need to be sent in writing because they are too long or complex to be easily assimilated on the telephone then make a 'telephone appointment' to discuss the quotation. 'I will send the figures today, what time will it be convenient for you to discuss them?' The customer will almost certainly have questions once he has assimilated the prices – it is important that you are available to answer them.

Customer: 'Right.'
Salesperson: 'OK?'

Speaker   **Analysis**

Customer: 'Thanks very much.'
Salesperson: 'No problem at all. Thanks.'
Customer: 'Bye.'
Salesperson: 'Bye-bye.'

By now you will realize that outbound telephone contact with customers demands the same degree of preparation and professionalism as any of your other business activities. It is possible to overcome customers' negative perceptions of telephone selling if the strategies and methodologies which are outlined in this book are adopted. Customers will appreciate a company's proactive interest in their business or consumer needs. If a company already has an established relationship with a customer the customer will perceive this interest as added value to its products or services.

Companies who have already embarked on proactive telephone contact programmes have been delighted with the positive response of their customers and have achieved their objectives of consolidating relationships with customers and increasing sales. Outbound calling delivers extra sales and service to customers in a very cost-effective way. If a company receives calls from customers then it is time to take the next step. Customers will appreciate the interest and concern that a proactive call demonstrates. The outbound call will also enable companies to identify business opportunities before their competition does.

Index

163

Customer Clubs and Loyalty Programmes

A Practical Guide

Stephan A Butscher

For any company, large or small, the most effective protection against competition is long-term customer loyalty. And, as Stephan Butscher's step-by-step guide explains, the key to customer loyalty lies in identifying and offering your customers the right combination of financial and non-financial benefits.

Too many customer clubs or loyalty programmes fall at the first hurdle because they base too much emphasis on discounts and other financial benefits, or because the sponsoring company fails to identify the kind of benefits that have high enough perceived value amongst their customers.

Customer Clubs and Loyalty Programmes will take you through all the necessary steps to research, plan and launch a programme that builds and develops the relationship between you and your customers; it puts special emphasis on value measurement and selection of the right benefits; it will also enable you to integrate the loyalty programme into every part of your organization; to maximize the research value; and to measure the ongoing success of your strategy, developing and growing the programme as you go.

The book includes case studies from some of the most successful companies from the UK, Europe, Australia and the USA, including Volkswagen Club, Kawasaki Riders Club, Microsoft Advantage, Swatch The Club and many more.

Gower

Gower Handbook of Customer Service

Edited by Peter Murley

In a world dominated by look-alike products at similar prices, superior customer service may be the only available route to competitive advantage. This *Gower Handbook* brings together no fewer than 32 professionals in the field, each one a recognized expert on his or her subject. Using examples and case studies from a variety of businesses, they examine the entire range of customer service activities, from policy formulation to telephone technique.

The material is presented in six parts:

- Customer Service in Context
- Measuring, Modelling, Planning
- Marketing Customer Service
- The Cultural Dimension
- The Human Ingredient
- Making the Most of Technology

For anyone concerned with customer satisfaction, whether in the private or the public sector, the *Handbook* is an unrivalled source of information, ideas and practical guidance.

Gower

Gower Handbook of Marketing

Fourth Edition

Edited by Michael J Thomas

This new edition of a well-established *Gower Handbook* has been extensively revised and updated. Numerous chapters have been added, on subjects as diverse as relationship marketing and international marketing research, and there are many new contributors.

Part I reflects the need for a strategic view of the marketing function and looks in detail at information systems, planning, environment analysis and competitor analysis. Part II covers the organization of marketing, including recruitment, training, brand management and finance. Part III looks at product development (including services), and Part IV with distribution. The final Part examines a number of aspects of marketing where new developments are making a profound impact and casts fresh light on such familiar topics as advertising, sales promotion, direct mail and franchising.

The 36 contributors represent an immense range of expertise. They are all acknowledged leaders in their chosen field, with practical experience of marketing.

Gower

Handbook of Customer Satisfaction Measurement

Nigel Hill

With the current emphasis on service as a competitive tool, delivering customer satisfaction has become a key strategic issue. But there's only one group of people who can tell you what the level of customer satisfaction is in your business, and that's the customers themselves. Using worked examples and real-life case studies, Nigel Hill's comprehensive guide takes you step by step through the entire process, from formulating objectives at the outset to implementing any necessary action at the end.

Among the topics covered are questionnaire design, sampling, interviewing skills, data analysis and reporting, while a set of valuable appendixes points the way to sources of further information and support. The book will equip the reader both to carry out a survey themselves and to brief and monitor an external agency for optimum results.

Whether you are directly responsible for measuring customer satisfaction or simply need to understand the issues and methods involved, the *Handbook* represents an unrivalled source of knowledge and advice.

Gower